D23

Tabula Picta

Tabula Picta

Painting and Writing in Medieval Law

Marta Madero

Translated by Monique Dascha Inciarte and Roland David Valayre

Foreword by Roger Chartier

PENN

University of Pennsylvania Press

Philadelphia

Published by
University of Pennsylvania Press
Philadelphia, Pennsylvania 19104-4112

Printed in the United States of America on acid-free paper

10   9   8   7   6   5   4   3   2   1

Library of Congress Cataloging-in-Publication Data

Madero, Marta.
    [Tabula picta. English]
    Tabula picta : painting and writing in medieval law / Marta Madero ; translated by Monique Dascha Inciarte and Roland David Valayre ; foreword by Roger Chartier.
        p. cm. — (Material texts)
    Originally published in French as: Tabula picta : la peinture et l'écriture dans le droit médiéval, 2004.
    Includes bibliographical references and index.
    ISBN 978-0-8122-4186-0 (alk. paper)
    1. Copyright (Roman law) 2. Law, Medieval. 3. Law and art—Europe—History—To 1500. I. Inciarte, Monique Dascha. II. Valayre, Roland David. III. Title.
KJA2438.I58M3713 2009
346.04'820902—dc22   2009023571

Contents

Foreword
The Things and the Words

Subtle and erudite, Marta Madero's book is a contribution both to the history of the *property* rights to artistic works and to the history of ideas about material things. The corpus that she so meticulously analyzes is that of the glosses and commentaries that medieval jurists consecrated to the question of *tabula picta*, a notion inherited from Roman law and the terms of which are seemingly simple: To whom does a painted tablet belong? To the owner of the physical piece of wood on which an image is painted? Or to the person who made the painting on that piece of wood? By extension, the same question could be formulated in regard to writing and the parchment or any other surface on which words had been inscribed.

It is thus possible to read Madero's book in the first instance by placing it in the genealogical longue durée of the definition of intellectual property and its corollary, the construction of the figure or—to use Foucault's formulation—function of the author. Such a reading finds, in the writings of the medieval jurists, the first formulations of a distinction made in the eighteenth century and articulated with particular clarity by Kant between the book as "opus mechanicum," as an object belonging to whoever has acquired it, and the book as discourse addressed to the public and remaining the inalienable property of the author who has written it. In their way, the medieval glossators also address the possible conceptual separation between works, considered in their immaterial and continuing identity, and the multiple forms, whether simultaneous or serial, of their inscription and transmission. Such an understanding of the book will see in the medieval distinction between *substantial essence* and *accidental forms* the opposition, dear to practitioners of physical bibliography, between "substantives" and "accidentals" and will recognize, as well, in the primacy given to the painted work over the materiality of the surface on which it is painted something like the concept of the "immatieral thing" framed in the eighteenth century to designate the transcendence of aesthetic or intellectual creations over their material existence. Such a reading of Madero's book is entirely legitimate but may, nevertheless, be misleading.

For in fact, Madero's book introduces us to an intellectual world that is neither ours nor that of the eighteenth century, when the aesthetic and legal concepts that have defined our modern discourse first came together. The danger would be to subsume wrongly and unconsciously the reasoning of the medieval jurists into the categories we have come to accept. For the medievals, the purpose above all was to situate things—whatever they might be—within a logical framework that allowed them to be described, categorized, and placed in a proper hierarchical order. Physical evidence, shared experience, the direct perception of natural or artificial realities are inadequate to this task because they are incapable of deconstructing and placing in proper order the individual elements that nature or human art has brought together into a single unit. Only juridical reasoning, which proceeds by way of establishing distinctions, taxonomies, and hierarchies, is capable of transforming the things before our eyes into manipulable categories that enable us to determine their real identities, properties, and ownership.

Important consequences emerge from this, which oblige us to abandon our habitual way of thinking about things if we are to understand how the authors whom Madero studies actually thought. For them, the painted tablets or sheets of parchment covered with writing are objects that can be comprehended only when one places them in the context of natural phenomena or material productions that pose the same questions about the relation between the parts and the whole, about the modes of uniting elements, or about the hierarchy of the matrix to that which appears upon it. I will leave to the reader the pleasure of discovering both the many subtle distinctions between things *factae* and *infactae*, between *accessio* and *specificatio* or *ferruminatio* and *adplumbatio*, as well as the multiplicity of opinions concerning the definition of these categories and the way they are handled in legal arguments. Madero's analytic virtuosity here is astounding, as she guides her reader through a universe of classificatory systems worthy of Borges. In truth, these address a hugely difficult task: that of articulating the essential reality to be decoded beneath visible appearances.

Madero thus takes the distinctions and categories of medieval law no less seriously than Yan Thomas did Roman law or Alain de Libera and Alain Boureau did Scholasticism; and her approach enables us to avoid two pitfalls. The first would be to connect too closely the *thought about the things* and legal procedural practice. The subjects of juridical argument are fully concrete, to be sure, as they concern financial transactions, the transfer of goods, and property disputes. But the construction of the categories that enabled the *jurists* to think about things is built upon a foundation of ancient and scholastic philosophy. It is governed neither by the urgency of the judgments nor by contractual relations between *patrons* and painters or copyists. The contractual matters that engage them take up none of the logic encountered in discussions of the *tabula picta* and focus, rather, on deadlines to be observed, payments to be made, and the details of the commission, such as the materials to be used, the iconography of the image, the typology of the *writing*. By focusing on the conceptual architecture of the glosses and commentaries rather than on the legal proceedings and decisions, Madero's approach runs counter to that by which historians, no doubt bored by the formalism of legal studies, have privileged actual judicial proceedings, legal practice, and the adjudication of disputes. She by no means intends to deny the importance of such studies, based as they are on the archival records of law courts. But her purpose here, as in her other published work in French and Spanish,[1] is to recall that in every period—and quite spectacularly so in the Middle Ages—law consists first of all in the conceptual description of acts, things, and people and that it is only upon this abstract description that legal judgments can be based.

A second eror would be to think that painting and writing were being considered by medieval jurists in aesthetic or intellectual terms. In the discussions concerning *tabula picta*, writing is always to be construed in its most material sense. It is inscription, *ductus*, and copy. It is never understood in the sense of literary composition even if the words *écrire* and *écrivain* have been used in French to describe authors as well as scribes since the fourteenth century. If the painting of wooden tablets has a different status, and one that implies the recognition of an original production, it is nevertheless not taken for a work of art. Its value is acknowledged according to the degree to which a rough material is transformed into a new object. The *tabula picta* as well as the written parchment belongs to the world of material objects, and not to that of aesthetic creation or symbolic representation.

The responses of the glossators to the question of the ownership of painted tablets or written objects varied from one school, period, or opinion to another, and Madero knowledgeably reconstructs the typology and chronology of these differences. She shows that however diverse they were, these responses were necessarily situated within a limited range of theoretical possibilities, defined by the logic of *accesio* and *significatio*. The first determines which of two materialities joined in a single object appertains to or incorporates the other, thus establishing the proprietary right. For some jurists, faithful to the *Institutiones* of Justinian, painting incorporates the wooden tablet, thus granting proprietary rights to the painter, while writing for its part is always subordinate to its matrix, whatever that may be, thus granting proprietary rights in the *litterae* to the owner of the *charta* on which they are traced or inscribed. The second logic ties proprietary rights to the creation of a new *species*, and grants them to whoever has, through a series of connected operations, created something new out of a raw material. Painted tablets could thus be considered by the logic of *specificatio*, at least when that which was painted on them met the criteria used to define a new *species*. Writing, on the other hand, was not thought of in these terms until it was assimilated into painting and its *value enhanced*; at that point, certain glossators came to reconsider writing too as a creative transformation of its matrix. Here again, Madero's finely honed analysis, attentive to the multiple figures who produced the overlapping or the hierarchical ordering of these two logics, offers a fine introduction to the ways of thought of medieval jurists, so alien to the reader of today.

That which has set them at such a distance from us, over and above their own intellectual methods, is doubtless the invention of modes for the mechanical reproduction of texts and images. For the medievals, each tablet or manuscript brought together, in a singular and unique manner, a matrix—of wood or parchment—and a painted image or a written text. This fundamental unity, which is altered with each new painting or each new manuscript copy, grounds the particularities of the arguments they used to define the character—accessory or essential, secondary or primary—of one or the other of the two materials indissolubly and specifically bound together in a single object. Mechanical reproduction shifts the terms of the argument, because it allows for the dissemination of the "same" text or the "same" image through the multiple physical objects—printed copies or engraved plates—that serve as their medium. The question of ownership thus shifts from the primacy of one element over another in a single object to the criteria by which one can recognize, in the multiplicity of the material forms of its inscription, a single "work," and thus a single creative inspiration—which now stands as the basis for proprietary rights.

It is because Marta Madero so lucidly and forcefully delineates this profound discontinuity that her book is much more than a scholarly and original study of one of the questions that pitted medieval jurists against one another by means of citations of authority, erudite glosses, and conceptual distinctions. *Tabula Picta* demonstrates, in effect, that the category of the materiality of the text—the unifying concern of the series in which *her* book now appears—is subject to historical variations that depend not only on the availability of particular techniques or materials. Perhaps even more, it is subject to the variable and plural categories that enable us, in different registers of experience and practice, to provide names, order, and attributions to things.

Roger Chartier
Translation by Jerome E. Singerman

Introduction

Who is the owner of a painting? He who painted the figures or he who owns the wood tablet on which the painter applied colors? Who is the owner of a written object? He who owns the parchment or he who wrote the text? From the twelfth century and until the end of the Middle Ages, jurists have debated these issues which seem very odd to us. Over the centuries, they have accumulated arguments and garnered references to support one position or the other. And, after them, legal historians have focused on this issue, traditionally known as that of the *tabula picta*.

Why revisit this classical issue today, in a book that would like to be more than a study in legal history? There are two reasons. The first relates to the long history of property rights over creative works, the landmarks of which should be kept in mind: in the last centuries of the Middle Ages, the emergence of the "book" in its modern form, which gathers the work (or works) of a single author in a single object, thus breaking away from the model of the miscellany, dominant from the seventh century on, which gathered texts very different in genre and nature into a single codex;[1] at the beginning of the modern era, the assigning of the texts to their authors for purposes of condemnation and prohibition, which Michel Foucault termed the penal appropriation of the discourse;[2] in the eighteenth century, the appearance, within guild rules in England or royal privilege in France, of the concepts of copyright and literary property.[3]

Revisiting the texts of ancient jurists means extending the genealogy upstream, with a focus on the rationales that allowed the transfer of property rights from the ownership of the material (parchment or wood tablet) to the work it supports, a written text or a painted work. Even if, in the Middle Ages, he who writes the text rarely is the author of the work—as the distinction between the work of the copyist and the invention of the author (as we understand it today) is profound—the legal texts nonetheless elaborate a first distinction between the materiality of the object and the intrinsic nature of aesthetic or intellectual productions.

The second reason for our inquiry goes beyond the sole issue of the *tabula picta*. In effect, the subtle disputes of medieval jurists on this issue open up a universe of strange and surprising thoughts. Their discourse is about concrete, material things and articulates categories and dichotomies built according to a very specific technical logic. Humanist and modern authors have often mocked those rationales, which link premises and consequences at a radical distance from common experience. However, in doing so, they reveal their imperfect knowledge. Indeed, the medieval gloss is in no way arbitrary or incoherent. It aims at formulating the principles necessary to characterize and classify things, and thus to subject them to legal operations. In order to allow sales or purchases, enjoyment of usufruct, transmission to heirs or legatees of rights over land, water, plants, buildings, and all kinds of manufactured objects, those things had to be envisaged in terms of resemblance or difference, wholes or parts, junctions and disjunctions. Evidence of the senses is insufficient to ground rights. Against their deceptive immediacy, legal discourse builds up the concepts and arguments of what one might call the artifice of the concrete. It permits the allocation of enjoyment rights over parts of a thing which, nonetheless, cannot be dismembered, and thus protects someone's property rights over the beam of a house or the arm of another's statue; or separates the purple from the garment, the belly from the body of a pregnant woman, roots from the totality of the tree, pure wheat from mixed grains, and painting from its support. The study of a specific example of the workings of these categories—here, the debate over the ownership of painted or written objects—gives access to the thought processes typical of medieval glosses that left durable imprints on the law. Moreover, it also allows us to observe an important moment in the development of the technique that established legal relationships between men and things. The goal thus is to contribute to the elaboration of a legal anthropology; however—contrary to the studies that focus on judicial processes and sociological dynamics accounting for the resolution of conflicts in a given society—the present work focuses on the technical processes specific to a modal understanding of the experiences and practices which, together, subjects them to the logical articulation of legal categories and gives them a reality removed from the evidence of the senses.

This book thus aims to fit a double perspective: a history of property rights over creative works and a history of thought as it relates to things. Switching from one to the other became a necessary process. Roger Chartier had proposed that I present the legal reach of texts written in the Middle Ages at the Oslo Historical Sciences Congress, in August 2000. At a seminar on labor in Roman law at the École des Hautes Études en Sciences Sociales, I had heard Yan Thomas speak briefly of the *tabula picta* and found what he had said fascinating. Reading the Roman and medieval texts, I realized they seemed to turn inside out the statement of the famous New Zealand bibliographer Donald F. McKenzie, who stated, in his first Panizzi Lectures at the British Library, that "the task of the bibliographer is to show that forms effect meaning." This remark, which opened up an entire field of research that sought to understand how the material forms of written objects relate to the construction of their meaning, could, to my mind, be reversed: "meaning effects forms," and this inversion could allow us to characterize the Roman law gloss and commentary writers' conception of the materiality of written or painted objects.

The medieval file of the *tabula picta* evidenced how the legal categories constantly reformulated the classifications based on variable and crossed opposites; and the plurality of those rationales signaled that materiality was not a given. To say, however, that it is nothing more than a construction of discourse would immediately lead us onto the classic and somewhat exhausted grounds of the relativist debate. I will thus try to be clear and, to do so, will resort to Michael Baxandall's book, *Giotto and the Orators,*[4] in which he shows that the Latin categorizations of experience, salvaged and learned like a foreign language by the humanists, influence not only manners of speech but also the very manner of seeing paintings, as they offer concepts that focus the attention. Legal language partly functions like the neoclassical Latin of the humanists: "it was never intended as a breathless statement of fresh perceptions of the world."[5] As with every language, its application to "some area of activity or experience . . . overlays the field after a time with a certain structure."[6] This does not lead to a rejection of reality. It would be more appropriate to say that, like all languages, the lawyer's "is a conspiracy against experience in the sense of being a collective attempt to simplify and arrange experience into manageable parcels."[7] It is only in that sense, I believe, that one may speak of materiality as a construction of the discourse.

Throughout the Middle Ages, Roman law gloss and commentary writers inscribed the *tabula picta* issue into complex categories that structured the relationship between materials and *species*: to be one, to take root, to unite, to blend, to mix, to prevail. They posited rationales that governed the substances, the forms of value, and the relationship between wholes and parts.

What we today call the legal renaissance of the twelfth century constitutes one of the major intellectual hinges in Western history. This movement, associated to the foundational moment of Irnerius's teaching in Bologna from the beginning of the twelfth century, was prepared by the Gregorian reform. Doctrinal thinking then developed around the legal *corpus* compiled in Byzantium by order of Emperor Justinian (sixth century) penetrates the West and serves as foundation, along with the development of canon law, for a normative discourse common to the European region. All the works we will cite belong to this monumental *corpus* generated between the seventh and fifteenth centuries.[8] With respect to the difference between gloss and commentary, one often cites the gloss proposed by grammarian Huguccio (twelfth century): "Glossa est expositio sententiae et ipsius literae, quae non solum sententiam sed etiam verba attendit" (the gloss is the explanation of a formula and of its very letter: it is interested not only in the formula but also in its terms); whereas the commentary is an "expositio verborum iuncturam non considerans sed sensum" (explanation of terms that takes into account not their alliance, but their meaning), quoted by Francesco Calasso.[9] One could say the gloss is an exegetic practice that "adheres" to the words and follows the order of the phrases—besides, we find them in the very margins of the pages of the manuscripts and of the later printed editions—whereas the commentaries are independent from it. The genre of the gloss dominates legal practice until the middle of the thirteenth century, in particular in the great school of Bologna. It was then replaced by the commentary. All the legal texts we will cite belong either to the gloss, or to the commentaries or *lecturae*, or finally to the *summae*, a genre that was widely popular outside of Bologna during the twelfth century. This variegated set of texts thus posited the issue of writing and painting in their most absolute materiality, but, due to the instability of the readings, it showed that no materiality was capable of imposing a logic inscribed within itself by nature. If the work of historians of books and reading has shown that real objects in which a text or an image crystallize, become visible or legible, impose constraints and take part in the elaboration of their meaning, we see here that materiality does not obey a necessary logic. It goes without saying that this approach is not meant to deny the pertinence of Donald F. McKenzie's affirmation. It is meant, on the contrary, to show its heuristic fertility by forcing us to ponder the diverse conceptions that have linked aesthetic and intellectual productions and their supports. In effect, if we can regard the *tabula picta* as a distant fragment from an archaeology of the rights of authors, we will see that the series thus constituted is very surprising.

Painting and writing, as envisaged by medieval jurists, bear on what happened when someone applied color or ink on a surface, *tabula* for the painting, *charta* or *membrana* for the writing. It was then necessary to decide which dominated by absorbing the other, to the extent that casuistry assumed the support and what was added to it belonged to different persons. It is, therefore, a discussion about the relationship between painting, writing, and their respective supports, about which one can already identify three characteristics: first, art or technique will not always be at issue; second, the contents of the writings will simply be irrelevant. There is an exception to this rule: a text by Ulpian (third century), D.10.4.3.14, which raises the issue of the supports used to write official acts. In this case, the rule that the support absorbs the writing does not necessarily apply. About this rule, Alberico de Rosate (✝ 1360)[10] states:

Mirabile verum, quod si in charta tua est scriptum magnum creditum meum quod scriptura cedat chartae [. . .] Alii dicunt quod in hoc casu ubi est magnum creditum dominus chartae non dicat, sicut nec dominus tigni iniuncti. Ne urbs deformetur.

[It would be truly extraordinary that, if your *charta* bears the inscription of an important debt I contracted, writing should appertain to the *charta*! (. . .) Some say that in the case of an important debt, the owner of the *charta* has no claim, nor does the owner of incorporated construction timber, to avoid the disfigurement of the city.]

Third, for some, the object of pictorial representation will be a significant criterion.

Indeed, the jurists envisaged painting and writing within a conceptual framework that was either the relationship between materials, or the tensions between *materia* and *species* (a term one can often translate as "specific thing," and very rarely as "form," but the complexity of which, in the medieval world, should not be overlooked),[11] or the issue of price, a criterion that tended to cut short the debate on the logic of materials.

When they spoke of writing and painting, medieval jurists commented on a file composed of texts compiled by order of Emperor Justinian in Byzantium during the sixth century. For purposes of this study, we are interested only in Books 6 and 41 of the *Digest* and Book 2 of the *Institutes*, in which one finds a discussion of the modes of acquisition of the *dominium* ranging from the capture of wild animals or rights over tame ones so long as they are in the habit of returning to their abode, to islands born in a river, including increases of the riparian domain when the river ebbs; delivery; or usufruct . . . Moreover, painting and writing were always approached using categories that dilated the subject and circumscribed a Borgesian universe, since the list of objects that could include writing and painting also included soil or trees carried by the river, plants and grains, buildings, the uniting of metals, the growth of fruits, construction timber, purple or the sleeves added to a garment, or gold threads or rows of pearls woven into a fabric . . .

Yet legal texts had an objective: to determine who owned the object. Therefore, they resorted to procedural rules dominated by two main lines of argument: on the one hand, all that relates to the criterion of *bona fides* in the subjects' actions; and, on the other, principles that respond to a way of thinking about things and materials.[12] Indeed, one of the main criteria of the judgment is the *bona fides* of he who applied those substances over a support that was not his;[13] and to this idea—which does not refer to a moral criterion, but to the state of mind of the subject when he is performing a given activity—should be added other manifestations of the disposition of the subjects that the law takes into account in order to adjudicate, such as two owners' common willingness to mingle materials they owned separately to create a common *acervus*, or deciding what should be regarded as principal or accessory in an object.

For the Romanists, in fact, the *tabula picta* raises an issue very many authors have tackled. It is what Vincenzo Arangio-Ruiz has called the *guazzabuglio gaiano*.[14] The *Institutiones* (2.78) of Gaius, a second-century jurist, offer contradictory propositions: if painting is in the hands of the *dominus tabulae*, the painter can get it back by paying the price of the *tabula*; if it is in the hands of the painter, the judge will return it to the *dominus tabulae* who paid the *impensa picturae*. In sum, he who is in possession of the thing is bound to lose it, which goes against the general criterion "possession is worth more than a claim." It also contradicts the rule by which "tabula picturae cedere" (the *tabula* appertains to the painting). Among others, Rudolph von Jhering and Pietro Bonfante have dealt with this issue, which concerns the *actiones* and has led to a hunt for interpolations in order to resolve the contradictions among the various texts.[15] Francesco Lucrezi submits that neither Gaius 2.78 (a manuscript from the second half of the fifth century), nor D.41.1.9.2, nor I.2.1.34 reflect the jurist's thoughts, and that the principle by which the *tabula* should appertain to the painting, which according to the author evidences the "victory of the artist," emerged not before the second half of the fifth century (p. 254). This could be confirmed by the statement of the *Epitome Gai*, drafted during the second half of the fifth century, which subjects painting to the principle governing writing, that is "what is above the soil is incorporated into the soil" (p. 32).[16] In this book, I will not address procedure and will also leave aside issues of will and intent. I will rather try to show the extraordinary diversity of what can be said about one aspect of materiality: that concerning the union of things and substances, the tensions between *materia* and *species*. I am mostly interested in understanding the multiple configurations associated with these acts (painting and writing), inextricably made part and parcel of a debate on the way things "behave."

The architecture of the sources justifies this approach, which differs from that of Paola Maffei, the author of the sole work exclusively dedicated to the *tabula picta* in the work of the gloss writers.[17] She states, like Francesco Lucrezi before her for the classical and postclassical Roman period, that the *tabula picta* raises not only a legal issue, but also an issue in the social history of art.[18] One cannot disagree with her about the role painting and sculpture played as modes of production of images in the Middle Ages, which also had the social function of bringing multiple messages—religious, political, and moral—to illiterate populations, and which, due to the number of those who could not read, are equally if not more important than writing. Guillaume Durand, in his famous *Rationale divinorum officiorum*, said that images are "laicorum littere" (the writing of the lay people),[19] and being seen, they have greater emotional power than writing, which is linked to hearing.[20] In this largely illiterate culture of the manuscript, the importance of writing and painting causes Paola Maffei to hold that the *tabula picta*, during the Middle Ages and up until the invention of the printing press, must not be regarded as a rare and complex textbook used to train the mind rather than to adjudicate but, on the contrary, as a debate on a concrete and practical issue.

Indeed, both the painter and the scribe were regarded as craftsmen rather than as artists, generally working on commission according to specific instructions; and the *pretiositas* criterion, which allowed many authors to take side for the painter or the writer, reveals a concern for labor. However, one should not forget that the issue of the *tabula picta* was never considered within the framework of a task performed by contract, because there is hardly any reference to the figures of *locator* and *conductor*. In these texts, the *dominus tabulae* or *chartae* is not the funding party,[21] and in this respect the *tabula picta* raises a less obviously practical issue than Paola Maffei asserts.

The *tabula picta* is a textbook case that is useful in thinking about the relationship between humans and things—according to logic different from that of the work contract—and about the things themselves. The separation between contract casuistic and that of the logic specific to painting and writing is so clear that Odofredo († 1265)—whose *lecturae* to the *Digest* are fundamental in the *tabula picta* file—manages in his *lectura* at D.45.1.72.1 to eulogize the scribes whose art exceeds that of the painters and at the same time to say, in the context of *locatio* and *conductio* contracts, that all copyists are "latrones et baratores."[22] By this, I do not mean to suggest that the *tabula picta* issue played no part in the practice, but it cannot be linked to work contracts, not only because it is removed from them by doctrine, but also because the *locatio operarum* contracts (in which the object is the term provisions of a work), and the *locatio operis* contracts (in which the object is the finished work) do not advance arguments specific to the *tabula picta*.

Rainiero de Perugia's *Ars notaria*, written in the 1220s, describes the *locatio operarum* formula, in which the funding party—*locator*—gives the scribe—*conductor*—the *exemplar* to be copied and provides him with the paper, a down payment, and a stipulation for two additional payments.[23]

De locationibus operum ad scribendum. Dominus Guido de Certona dedit et locavit ad scribendum unum Digestum Vetus Martino de Fano hoc modo et pacto, quod dictus dominus nec per se nec per alium ipsi scriptori auferret dictum opus nisi prius ab eo finiatur, et pro mercede dicti operis dabit eidem Martino prefatus dominus Guido x lib. bon., medietatem in principio operis, aliam medietatem expleta ipsius operis medietate, et cartas dabit ei ad scribendum ad sufficientiam quandocumque petet, et exemplar vel cartas habeat quando expediet preparatas, ita quod dictus scriptor non amittat opus; et si amiserit eo quod non exemplar vel cartas non habeat quando expediat preparatas, totum damnum debet ei dominus resarcire. Et dictus Martinus debet dicto domino Guidoni scribere et explere continue totum Digestum Vetus de adeo tam bono testo sicut ei demonstravit in quodam quaterno domini Iohannis Parisiensis, nisi forte acciderit occasione temporis vel cartule vitiose, bona fide, sine alicuius alterius operis scripture interpositione excedentis quantitatem x sol. bon., et rubricas et minora remittet ei secundum consuetudinem huius terre. Que omnia inter se ad invicem stipulantes promiserunt per se suosque heredes attendere ac servare; nec contra per se vel alium venire vel facere aliqua occasione vel exceptione: et sumptus omnes reficere, et expensas in iuditio vel extra sub pena c sol. bon.

[Work contracts for a work of writing. Master Guido de Certona has hired the services of Martinus de Fano and has given him the *Digestum Vetus* to be transcribed in one copy by a contract drafted as follows: said master shall not, neither personally nor through the agency of another, withdraw said work from the appointed scribe so long as it is not finished; the aforementioned master Guido shall, for said work, give said Martinus a salary of ten Bolognese pounds, one half on inception of the work, the other half when said work shall be finished; he will furnish him with writing paper in a sufficient quantity every time he will be asked; said scribe shall have the original and the paper in his possession upon finishing that given him, in order not to renounce the work; if he renounces it because he has neither the original nor the paper when he finishes that given him, the master must indemnify him entirely. As for said Martinus, he must transcribe to the end and without interruption the entirety of the *Digestum Vetus*, in a penmanship as beautiful as that shown to him on a *quaternion* by master Jean de Paris; if perchance circumstances associated with the delay or the bad quality of the paper prevent him from doing so, when he is in good faith and has meantime performed no additional writing work, he will remit the sum of ten *soldi*, the red inks, and the objects of lesser value pursuant to this country's custom. The parties to the contract solemnly promised each other in their name and in the name of their legatees to acknowledge and abide by all these clauses; not to violate or breach them, personally or through the agency of another, under any circumstance or exception; to bear all costs as well as expenses in case of a lawsuit or additional costs under penalty of a one-hundred *soldi* fine.]

In Rolandino Passaggeri's *Summa totius artis notariae*, written in the 1260s, one finds the most common version among writing contracts in which the funding party holds, on the contrary, the part of the *conductor*, and the scribe that of the *locator*: the contract *locatio operis*.[24]

Hoc instrumentum locationis operarum ad opus scripture faciendum distinguitur per tres partes. Nam in prima locator paciscitur conductori scribere unum ff. vetus in textu de tali litera, ut ei ostendit in tali quaterno, et bene continuare literam praedictam, et hoc pro certa quantitate, cuius quantitatis partem iam confitetur habere locator. In secunda parte instrumenti conductor se obligat locatori ad residuum mercedis certo modo et tempore solvendum.

[This formula of *locatio operis* for a work of writing breaks down into three tiers. In the first tier, the *locator* commits to transcribe for the benefit of the *conductor* the *Digestum Vetus* in penmanship similar to what he showed him on a similar *quaternion*, to properly apply without interruption said penmanship, all for a specified sum, a part of which the *locator* acknowledges he has already received. In the second tier of the instrument, the *conductor* warrants he will pay the *locator* the rest of his salary at a specified date and according to specified terms.]

Writing contracts for the copying of legal books in Bologna, as analyzed by Luciana Devoti,[25] exhibit some diversity, but they are generally entered into for the totality of the work and specify a price per *quaternus*. For example, a contract signed in 1265 to "scribere totum apparatum Digesti veteris in glosa" (transcribe in its entirety the apparatus of the *Digestum Vetus* in the form of a gloss) specifies a unit price of 216 *bolognini* per *quaternus*—the division of the texts in *quaternus* corresponded to the official division in the scholarly world—and a total price of 9,120 *bolognini*. Out of four contracts for the copying of the gloss to the *Infortiatum*, only one, signed in 1269, proposes a global price of 13,440 *bolognini*; in the three others, the price set per *quaternus* is 180 *bolognini* in 1269, and 264 and 288 in 1270. Some funding parties pay little but agree to furnish lodging and food for the contract duration.[26]

According to the University bylaws, all the trades related to the book in

Bologna were subject to strict oversight.[27] The contracts used in Bologna have characteristics related to the *studium* constraints and tend to omit certain issues that could be raised outside of this particular milieu, such as the scribe's power to withhold the already copied *quaterni* if the funding party does not pay, even when the unpaid amount is relatively unimportant. A form drafted by Leo Speluncanus dating from the mid-fourteenth century, generated outside of the intellectual milieu of Bologna and thus unconstrained by the *studium* interests, elucidates some issues raised by this type of contract. He ponders four topics:

Oppono contra instrumentum, et dico, quod talis contractus est uenditionis, et emptionis, quia ubicumque interuenit pretium, est emptio, et uenditio [...] Resp. uerum est, quod ubicumque interuenit pretium, est emptio, et uenditio, tamen quandocumque pro pretio promittitur aliquid faciendum, ut in caso nostro, est locatio [...] Vlterius quaero, ecce, quod isti scriptori fuissent solutae per istum Sempronium conductorem, qui fecit fieri istum codicem, unciae quinque, et de uncia una esset residuum, posset iste scriptor retinet totum istum codicem pro illa uncia, quousque erit sibi soluta? Resp. potest [...] Secus in libro exempli secundum Bar. [...] Vlterius quaero, ecce, quod iste S. qui faciebat fieri istum librum, fuit mortuus, priusquam fieret liber iste, potuerunt dicere heredes istius S. huic scriptori, nolimus, quod facias nobis istum librum? Resp. non [...] Vlterius quero, iste scriptor potuisset scribere istum librum per subsitutum.s. per unum alium, et non scriberet ipse scriptor? Resp. non.

[I have one objection against this form and affirm that such a contract is a purchase and sale contract, since every time price intervenes, there is purchase and sale. (...) Response: It is correct that there is purchase and sale every time price intervenes, yet each time a work is promised for a price, as in the instant case, it is a *locatio* (...). I further ask the following: assuming five *unciae* were paid to the scribe by Sempronius, the *conductor* who ordered the work, but one *uncia* remains owed, could the scribe withhold the entire work as security until that *uncia* was paid? Response: Yes. (...) It is otherwise, according to Bartolo, with respect to the exemplar. (...) I further ask as follows: said Sempronius, who ordered this book, died before said book was completed; could his heirs have said to the scribe: "We refuse that you do it for us"? Response: No. (...) I further ask whether the scribe could have had the book transcribed by his substitute or by another scribe, instead of transcribing it himself? Response: No.][28]

On the contrary, the university environment tended to stress the serious breach of the scribe who failed to deliver his work. Rainiero Arsendi da Forlì— a character of great notoriety born toward the end of the thirteenth century, a professor in Bologna and later in Pisa and Padua where he lived until his death in 1358—proposed that the guilty copyist be likened to a debtor of the state. However, it is Signorolo degli Omodei, a fortunately obscure disciple of Rainiero da Forlì's, who expressed the most radical condemnation by associating writing work with *honor ciuitatis*: the copyist could be condemned to decapitation: [29]

Imo posset argui quod deberent decapitari et sic propter inopiam librorum veritas celatur, hinc est quod antiquis temporibus pauci ex multis perficiebant lites suas [. . .] Propterea commitens circa libros legales uidetur esse dignus pena capitis.

[Better, one could demonstrate they should be decapitated, in that, in the absence of books, the truth remains hidden. For this reason, in ancient times, out of a large number of people, only a small number litigated to the end (. . .) This is why, guilty with respect to legal books, he seems to deserve capital punishment.] [30]

This opinion was not followed by more recent jurists, and the seriousness of the fault concerns only public-interest books, that is to say books regarding the law, medicine, or other scientific matters. One can therefore attest to the fact that neither the doctrine nor the notarial forms nor the executed contracts refer to the rationales specific to the *tabula picta*.

The same applies to painting. The commission contracts (*prix-faits*), that is the contracts entered into for the execution of a work stipulating the conditions of its realization and its price, are very diverse as to the more or less precise description of the work to be accomplished[31]—subject, position of the images, colors, presence and quality of the gilding, preparation of the support, relationship to models seen by the funding party—and as to the modes and forms of payment—generally divided into a down payment at the outset, a second payment in the course of the work, and a last payment upon delivery of the finished work. The clauses governing default in the execution of the work allow attachment of the property of the painter or restitution of the amount paid but, as in writing contracts, they do not articulate a rationale specific to the *tabula picta*.

As one example of the details commonly included in commission contracts, one can review the contract between Master Philippus Gactus, painter, and Dame Margareta de Blanco for paintings to be executed in the Santa Catarina Chapel inside her palace, done at Palermo, on January 2, 1349.

Magister Philippus Gactus, pictor, civis felicis urbis Panormi, presens coram nobis, locavit opera sua servicia sue persone nobili domine Margarete de Blanco ad pingendum quandam cappellam suam sitam et positam intus hospicium dicte domine vocatum Sancta Catherina ut infrascriptum est, videlicet quod primo et principaliter debet facere Salvatorem in tribuna dicte capelle et alias picturas quae necessarie fuerint. Item debet pingere conam unam de lignamine, de auro fino et azolino ultramarino et de omnibus aliis coloribus qui in dicta cona necessarie fuerint. Item debet facere sanctam Ursulam eo modo et forma prout est depicta in ecclesia Sancti Francisci. Item debet facere sanctam Elisabeth eo modo et forma prout est depicta in ecclesia Sancte Trinitatis, excepto quod non debet ponere follam de auro nisi in diadematibus et coronis tantum. Item debet pingere residuum dicte capelle ad voluntatem dicte domine in omni parte in qua expedierit [. . .] Item extra dictam capellam supra portam debet facere interlacos et in angulo facere sanctum Christoforum.

[Master Philippus Gactus, painter and citizen of the happy city of Palermo, before us, did rent his services to noble Dame Margareta de Blanco, to execute the paintings of a chapel located inside the palace of said lady and called Santa Catherina, as hereafter written: first and foremost, he must, on the gallery of said chapel, represent the Savior and execute the other necessary paintings. In addition, he must execute a wooden icon with pure gold, ultramarine blue and all the other colors necessary for said icon. In addition, he must represent Saint Ursula exactly as on the painting in Saint Francis Church. In addition, he must represent Saint Elisabeth exactly as on the painting of the Saint Trinity, except he must apply gold leaf on the diadems and crowns only. In addition, he must paint the rest of said chapel according to said lady's will in every instance where she gave instructions. (. . .) In addition, outside said chapel, he must paint entwined motifs above the door and represent Saint Christopher in the corner.][32]

The texts I will analyze range from the twelfth to the fifteenth century. They were written by Roman law gloss and commentary writers during the era commonly known as that of classical *ius commune*. My analysis ends with the emergence of legal humanism.[33] This periodization also corresponds to the dissemination of the printing press. Only Jason de Maino (1435–1519), whom I cite solely about the classification of *partes*, wrote after the dissemination of the printing press. The jurists I study thus share the common experience of manuscript culture. I do not mean to say this culture remained unchanged between the twelfth and the fifteenth century, and even less that it disappeared after Gutenberg; numerous recent studies demonstrate, on the contrary, the vitality of manuscript culture in the age of the printing press;[34] and a work such as that of Johannes Trithemius († 1516), the abbot of Sponheim, recalls with nostalgia the advantages of a manuscript culture that the unruly expansion of the printing press has marginalized. His arguments focus on:

—superior quality of parchment:

Sciptura enim, si membranis imponitur, ad mille annos poterit perdurare, impressura autem cum res papyrea sit, quamdiu subsistet? Si in volumine papyreo ad ducentos annos perdurare potuerit, magnum est.

[Indeed, if writing is applied on parchment, it will endure a thousand years, but a printed text, being on paper, how long will it endure? If a paper volume could last two hundred years, that would be a lot.]

—poor distribution of printed books, the freedom of the scribe who can evade constraints and censorship:

Non patitur constringi sub conditione impressoris. Liber est, et libertatis suae gaudebit officio.

[He does not have to bear constraining conditions imposed on him by the printer. He is free, and will rejoice in the freedom of his work.]

—lack of reliability of the printed book.[35]

However, the emergence of the printing press at least offers one alternative to the copyist.

Roman and medieval sources thus demonstrate that any history of artwork property implies a history of thought about things. The sources discuss the theme of the *tabula picta* in a context that does not always concern art and technique and, even when they do, the discussion addresses numerous forms of transformation of materials. The fragment (D.6.1.23) by Paul (second century) thus discusses the world of arts and techniques, as it mentions statues, vessels, tables, paintings and writings, things united by *ferruminatio*—welding in the same metal as that of the welded parts—or *adplumbatio*—welding in a material different from that of the welded parts—and construction materials. Yet the *Rerum cottidianarum* attributed to Gaius (second century) by Justinian compilers—actually the postclassical work of an unknown author—mentions slave escapees recovering their original freedom, things united by *alluvio* (everything the river removes from, or brings to, the riverbank fields), islands born of the sea, *specificatio* as a transformation process of things as diverse as grapes into wine, olives into oil, grains into flour, silver or gold into vessels, or wine and honey mixed into *muslum*. The text ends with the evocation of construction materials and, finally, plants.

In addition, when medieval jurists report the issues raised by those texts, they use categories that further broaden this world of things, materials, and *species*. The language and the rationales of the sources thus leads me to step back from any analysis too hastily focused on the craftsman and his production, as by doing so one settles too promptly into a modern approach to artistic and intellectual property, which raises a double issue: that of the legal identification of creation; and that of the assertion of property rights over it. My approach is of a different nature and proposes to return to the world of things, to the categories that allow us to formulate a number of relationships between humans and things, of which writing and painting—being acts and artifacts—are examples.

Chapter 1
Dominium *and Object Extinction*

When the issue is to know to whom a written or painted object belongs when the owner of the support and the owner of the inscriptions or motives are not the same person, things, at the outset, always come down to a determination of the *dominium*. However, under Roman law, the *dominium* is invested in the thing; it has the same destiny. If the thing disappears, if it becomes extinct under the law, so does the *dominium*. Such is the case for a metallic part, such as the handle of a vessel or an arm affixed to a statue, when the object as well as the part and the soldering metal were of the same nature—the mode of attachment the law called *ferruminatio.* If, on the contrary, the extinction is not definitive and there still exists a way of returning to the original object—for example by adding a stone to a ring, a plank to a boat, or an arm to a statue, albeit by using a metal different from the joint parts—a process known as *adplumbatio*—then, under certain conditions, the *dominium* does not perish because the object has retained its individual quality and has the potential to recover its autonomy sooner or later.

[Cassius] dicit enim, si statuae suae ferruminatione iunctum bracchium sit, unitate maioris partis consumi: et quod semel alienum factum sit, etiamsi inde abruptum sit, redire ad priorem dominum non posse. Non idem in eo, quod applumbatum sit: quia ferruminatio per eandem materiam facit confusionem, plumbatura non idem efficit.

[(Cassius) says in effect that if an arm was attached to its statue by *ferruminatio*, because of unity, it is absorbed into the greater part, and, once part of another's property, even if it (the arm) were later torn off, it would not return to the prior owner. Not so with what was *applumbatum*, because *ferruminatio* with the same substance causes fusion, whereas this does not happen with *plumbatura*.] (D.6.1.23.5)

Therefore the question asked was double. One had to decide, on the one hand, whether or not there was extinction of the object when the colors or the ink were applied to a support; and, on the other hand, which of the two, the support or the addition, became extinct. The thing could be regarded as having lost its individuality, its existence under the law, in two situations, which Roman law had not systematized, but which medieval law acknowledges as specific and classified forms of *dominium* acquisition: *accessio* and *specificatio*. They do not imply the systematic disappearance of the thing, but in many cases, they lead to it.

In order to understand the body of references that define the space of this reflection, I propose a description based upon two successive organizations of the sources. First, one must describe the framework of the *tabula picta* in Roman texts, strictly limiting the analysis to the passages that discuss it. At a second stage, one will have to consider the body constituted by the fragments in which writing and painting are discussed and to take into account the ordinary glosses of Accursio, who taught in Bologna between 1200 and 1263 and was a disciple of Azo's (ca. 1190–1220), the greatest master of his time. His large gloss, or ordinary gloss, which contains close to ninety-seven thousand fragments from various authors including himself, will become essential and will bring the era of the glosses to an end because of its authority, the genre being subsequently continued by *additiones* to his monumental compilation.[1]

Proceeding thus will allow us to establish a list of the themes that jurists mobilized in their attempt to circumscribe an evasive object; for if the fate of a rooted tree, of construction timber added to the house of another, of the progeny of animals, of mixed grains, or of metal masses seem to be governed by stable criteria, it is not the same for painting and writing.

In Book 6 of the *Digest*, Title 1, which discusses *Rei vindicatio*, contains a text by Paul, a jurist from the Severan period:

Sed et id, quod in charta mea scribitur, aut in tabula pingitur, statim meum fit: licet de pictura quidam contra senserint. propter pretium[2] picturae: sed necesse est ei rei cedi id, quod sine illa esse non potest.

[But what is written on my papyrus or painted on my board becomes mine immediately; perhaps some may be of a different opinion with respect to painting, because of the cost of paint, but a thing unavoidably appertains to that without which it cannot subsist.] (D.6.1.23.3)

A second text included in Title 1, *De adquirendo rerum dominio,* from *Digest 41,* an excerpt from the *Rerum cottidianarum,* contrasts writing, which must always belong to its support, just as what is built or planted belongs to the land, with painting which, to the contrary, incorporates the board it covers:

Litere quoque licet auree sint, perinde chartis membranisque cedunt, ac si solo cedere solent ea que aedificantur aut seruntur. Ideoque si in chartis membranisve tuis carmen vel historiam vel orationem scripsero: huius corporis non ego, sed tu dominus esse intellegeris.

[Letters, be they of gold, appertain to the papyrus or the parchment just like things that are built or planted customarily appertain to the land. And for that reason, if I write a poem, a story, or a speech on your papyrus or on your parchment, you will know that I am not the owner of that writing, you are.]

Sed non uti litere chartis membranisve cedunt, ita solent picture tabulis cedere: sed ex duerso placuit tabulas picture cedere.

[But the letters do not appertain to the papyruses or the parchments in the same manner as paintings customarily appertain to the boards: on the contrary, it is held that boards appertain to the paintings.] (D.41.1.9.1–2)

Finally, from a passage from Book 2 of Justinian's *Institutes* on the division of things and the manners of acquiring ownership of them, it is said that letters, even when drawn in gold, must appertain to their support, but not painting:

Literae quoque, licet aureae sint, perinde chartis membranisve cedunt, ac si solo cedere solent ea quae inaedificantur, aut inseruntur ideoque si in cartis, membranisve tuis carmen, vel historiam, vel orationem Titius scripserit: huius corporis, non Titius: sed tu dominus esse videris.

[Letters, be they of gold, appertain to the papyruses or to the parchments just like things that are built or sowed customarily appertain to the land. And for that reason, if Titius has written a poem, a story, or a speech on your papyruses or your parchments, it will appear to you that Titius is not the owner of that writing, but you are.]

Sid quis in aliena tabula pinxerit, quidam putant tabulam picturae cedere: aliis videtur, picturam, qualiscunque sit, tabulae cedere. sed nobis videtur melius esse, tabulam picturae cedere. Ridiculum est enim, picturam Apellis, vel Parrhasii in accessionem vilissimae tabulae cedere.

[If someone has painted on the board of another, some think that the board appertains to the painting, others think that the painting, whatever it may be, appertains to the board: but it seems to us, rather, that the board appertains to the painting. It would be nonsense, in truth, that a painting by Apelle or Parrhasios appertain *in accessionem* to a board of minuscule value.] (I.2.1.33–34)

First and foremost, a lexical caveat is necessary. The verbs *cedere* and *accedere*, as used in legal Latin, both translate into "appertain" and signify that one element or value is added to a thing, and thus becomes subordinate to it. In the present context, *cedere* and *accedere* both mean that the added value of the artist's or the scribe's work is incorporated to the *tabula* or the *charta*, or, on the contrary, incorporate its support. For the sake of clarity, I will, on occasion, give equivalents of this construction, which is specific to the legal language and does not exist in ordinary language, such as "absorb," "incorporate," or "dominate," and I will also highlight the differences between *cedere* and *accedere* when they are systematically and intentionally distinguished.[3]

The first framework of those fragments is thus governed by the principle *superficies solo cedit* (the surface appertains to the land): painting and writing must appertain to their support as things that are built, planted, or sowed appertain to the land; that is to say, all things which, absent their appurtenance, could not exist. And when the fragments depart from this principle to find that the *tabula* appertains to the colors, the argument is one of value. For classical and postclassical Roman law, writing never is capable of attracting the material of its support, even if the price of the substances used to write could justify such a conclusion. The value that is evoked when discussing painting, therefore, is not that of the painting materials, but that of the painter's work.

If we now take into account the ensemble where the issue of the *tabula picta* appears, the first text we just considered belongs to a commentary by Jurist Paul, in which, after having excluded from the claim things that cannot be incorporated in any person's patrimony—such as sacred and religious things—he enumerates the adjunction of one thing to another in such a way that the added thing becomes a part—such is the case when an arm is added to a statue, or a handle to a cup, or a leg to a table; writing and painting; construction timber and the *cementa* that pertain to the structure of a building. Those are, in fact, things joined or added according to three sorts of logic. A logic of *praevalentia*, which allows the determination of which of two things will appertain to the other—a criterion founded, for the gloss, on the relationship between the part and the whole, or on the value. A second logic that governs the forms of the adjunction (opposition between *ferruminatio* and *adplumbatio*). And, finally, a logic that, according to stoic physics, distinguishes between things that are simple, composite, or collective. The gloss adds two additional criteria Paul's fragment does not mention, but which already existed in the Justinian compilation: that of things that are *factae* and *infectae*, that of ornament.

Item loquitur hic quando factum facto argento iungitur: et fit eius pars. vbi autem infectum infecto, quilibet suae partis dominus permanet.

[We hold the same discourse when silver *factum* is joined to silver *factum*: it becomes part of the whole. But when a thing *infecta* is joined to another, each remains the owner of his separate part.] (D.6.1.23.2 *Adiecerit*)

In gemma autem annulo iniuncta distingue. quid cuius ornandi causa adiungatur.

[And in the case of a gem mounted on a ring, you must determine what was joined for ornamental purposes.] (D.6.1.23.4 *Per praeualentiam*)

The second passage we must take into account is the beginning of D.41.1.9, as well as paragraphs 1 and 2, which deal with things that coalesce (*coalescunt*). Beyond that, the document deals with a form of *dominium* acquisition by *traditio,* which does not concern the *tabula picta.* What is at issue here are the plants and grains that coalesce with the soil and are meant to appertain to the land from which they draw nutrients, the buildings that appertain to the land on which they are erected, the letters that appertain to the papyrus and parchments as erected buildings or sowed plants appertain to the soil (it is worth remembering that the medieval vocabulary relating to writing often uses words associated with planting and sowing—*inserere*—plowing, drawing a furrow—*exarare*).[4] And finally, of painting that, although no reason for it is provided in this passage, behaves differently from writing, since the *tabulae,* on the contrary, must appertain to the painting. The gloss adds one distinction between *accessio diuina* and *humana natura cooperante* in order to single out the plants borne by the winds or carried by waters (which are governed by *accessio divina*) from among those planted by humans:

Est haec accessio diuina et humana, natura cooperante. Idem si diuina tantum planta vel frumentum coaluit.

[There is an accession caused by God and an accession caused by man, seconded by nature. The same applies when a plant or grain becomes rooted solely through an act of God.] (D.41.1.9 *Conseuit*)

However, in both cases, the fact of coalescing with the soil results in an appurtenance of the plant to the soil, to which it becomes incorporated. The ordinary gloss also modifies the interpretation of the segment opposing painting to writing and assimilates writing to painting: from now on, the supportive medium of writing appertains to the writing, as the *tabula* appertains to the painting. Painting and writing both absorb their support.

Item quae est ratio diuersitatis in pictis et in scriptis? Respon. forte quia scriptores antiqui temporis non erant adeo cari sicut sunt hodie. vnde cum parui pretij esset scriptura, cedebat chartae: quae scilicet charta carior erat. econtrario pictores et fuerunt et sunt cari, et tabula vilijs pretij est et fuit: vnde cedit picturae secundum Io. Sed cum hodie sit scriptura pretiosior quam charta: potest idem quod in pictura dici, secundum Azo.[5]

[What is, on the other hand, the reason for this difference between painting and writing? Answer: it so happens that ancient *scriptores* were less valuable than those of today. Accordingly, since writing was lest costly, it appertained to the *charta*, which, conversely, was more expensive. By contrast, painters were and remain expensive, whereas a board costs little: therefore, according to Iohannes, it appertains to the painting. However, since nowadays writing is more costly than a *charta*, we may, according to Azo, say the same thing as in the case of a painting.] (D.41.1.9.1 *Directam vindicationem*)

The third passage, that of Justinian's *Institutes*, presents itself as follows. After mentioning plants, seeds, and buildings, it discusses writing and painting. Paragraph 35, however, leads to a different theme, that of "cultura et cura" (culture and care). The gloss will refer to Placentin's interpretation, which decides according to the nature of the represented thing—is it man or beast?—and to the quality of the pigments.[6] According to tradition, Placentin (✝ ca. 1200) was the first *doctor legum* to have taught at Montpellier, where he arrived, no doubt, around 1162. As a central figure of the Provençal schools recently studied by André Gouron,[7] he authored two *summae* that were fundamental for the *Codex* and the *Institutes*. Originally, the *summa* genre was typical of the French Midi schools, but it is also found in Bologna between the end of the twelfth century and the beginning of the thirteenth century. The word is not mentioned, but what is at issue here, as we will observe in Placentin's works, is the problem of the *specificatio*, that is to say the creation of a new *species*, a new "specific thing," which argues against the idea of adjunction in favor of a logic of transformation and creation.

We now can establish a first list of themes that will have to be developed in order to understand the different way jurists have to think about the relationship between writing, painting, and their supports. That list includes the fact of *coalescere*, for plants and buildings; *ferruminatio* and *adplumbatio*; categorizing things as simple, composite, or collective; the *factae et infectae* categories; *praevalentia*; value; the part and the whole; and ornament.

We must now move beyond this point. Upstream from the ordinary gloss, we must take into account a number of important texts, such as Placentin's—the most original one in its conception of *specificatio*—Azo's, or Jean Bassian's. Azo (✝ ca. 1230), the greatest master of his time, is the author of *summae* to the *Codex* and the *Institutes*, as well as a collection of *summulae* to the *Digest*. He also began a systematic review of the *apparatus* and thus prepared the *magna glossa*, which his disciple, Accursio, completed. Jean Bassian (✝ ca. 1193) taught in Bologna at the end of his life, with Azo as one of his disciples, and was also a professor in Mantua and probably in Cremona, his town of birth, or Piacenza. He is regarded as the man who renewed Bolognese tradition by introducing a dialectic method, which in turn led to the commentary genre.[8] Downstream, we must focus on what the authors of *lecturae* and *commentaria* say about those passages which, in the fourteenth and fifteenth century, are not the object of systematic commentaries, far from it. The first list we established is therefore enriched with two new citations we find in Bartolo—the relationship between liquid and dry things, the degree to which an area's surface is occupied, and—a theme developed at length by Angelo de Ubaldi—the opposition between *qualitas* and *substantia*.

Bartolo (1313–57), who enjoyed great notoriety toward the end of his short life, became truly legendary in the fifteenth century and after. He first studied in Perugia with Cino de Pistoia and obtained the title of doctor at twenty-one in Bologna. He practiced as an assessor in Todi and then as a prosecuting attorney in Macerata; he was intensely active in Pisa until 1342 and then in Perugia, where he died at forty-three in 1357. He is the most famous of all the commentators. His work was to be taught on a par with the *corpus iuris*.[9] Angelo de Ubaldi is the brother of the famous Baldus,[10] disciple of Bartolo. It is believed that the dates we use for his birth (1328) and death (1407) are approximations. He taught in various cities and is the author of commentaries to the *Digest* (see my chapter "*Qualitas* and *Substantia*" herein) and the *Codex*.[11]

However, we must first establish as a starting point the definition of two modes of acquisition of the *dominium* that Romanists have used to think about painting and writing: *accessio* and *specificatio*.

Accessio and *Specificatio*

As envisaged in the Middle Ages, *accessio* designates, on the one hand, cases where the owner of a thing acquires another from the sole fact that the second is the fruit of the first (children of a slave woman, the young of animals, fruits from trees), and on the other hand, the acquisition of things that become united. As a means of acquiring the *dominium, accessio* produces "the legal consequence of attributing to the owner of the thing ownership of what complements it, enriches it, or aggrandizes it."[12] There are numerous typical cases, such as building, planting and sowing of land, or joining metals or pieces of wood, which are, in effect, governed by the principle of *superficies solo cedit*. However, for the ensemble including *inaedificatio, plantatio*, and *satio*, if the land absorbs all that coalesces with it, the union of two movable objects is governed by the principle according to which a thing that is *accessoria* must appertain to that which is perceived as being principal; that is to say, the dominant element is that which assumes the function of the whole, and the subordinate thing is no more than its complement or ornament.

The *specificatio* designates the transformation of one thing into another, the birth of a new *species*, which does not translate into a form, but rather a thing, in the sense of individuality, or a set of characteristics that make it individual.[13] That transformation often takes place via human intervention, but not necessarily: it may derive from a process such as the dismantling of a ship as the result of a wreck or the combination of various elements (D.7.4.10.7, D.32.88.2, D.41.1.7.9.).[14] The issue raised by *specificatio* is to know who owns the new *species* when the owner of the thing and the one who transformed it are not the same person: the thing might be brand new, without legal existence before its transformation, which should thus belong to him who created it; or the thing might remain "substantially" the same because, without its original substance (the matter of which it is made), it would have no existence, and thus must belong to him who owned the material. Those two positions, identified as belonging to, respectively, the Proculians and the Sabinians,[15] will give rise to a *media sententia*: if the new *species* can be reduced to its core substance (such as the silver vessel that, once melted, reverts to a mass of silver), then it belongs to the *dominus materiae*; if, however, the specification process cannot be reversed (as in the case of oil, which can never be an olive again, or wine, which cannot revert to grapes), then it belongs to the agent of the *specificatio*.

It would be interesting to perform a systematic comparison between the legal texts and the commentaries to Aristotle's *Physics* and *Metaphysics*.[16] Thus, for example, the *naturalia et artificialia* categories, the manner in which one defines the existence of a *nova res* or the operations of *artifices* that can act by *substractio, compositio, transformatio*, sometimes even by the simple contact between substances acting of their own principle, could be compared to the manner by which medieval lawyers interpreted the *accessio*, the *specificatio*, and the avatars of materials and *species*. One example will suffice, which belongs to Aegidius Romanus's commentaries to the *Physics*:

Fiunt autem que fiunt simpliciter. Alia quidem transfiguratione: ut statua. Alia vero appositione: ut que augmentantur. Alia vero abstractione: ut ex lapide mercurius. Compositione autem ut domus. Alteratione vero: ut que conuertuntur secundum materiam. Omnia autem que sic fiunt: manifestum est: quoniam ex substantiis fiunt. Inducit in naturalibus et artificialibus simul dicens quod que fiunt simpliciter alia fiunt ex transfiguratione ut statua. alia ex appositione ut ea que augmentantur ut fluuius ex diuersis riuis. alia ex abstractione et ex remotione ut ex lapide.i.in lapide mercurius.i.forma mercurii. sculpitur per remotionem partium lapidis. alia fiunt compositione ut domus alia alteratione et transfiguratione: ut que conuertuntur adinuicem secundum naturam: ut ex aqua aer et econuerso. cum ergo in omnibus his aliquid subiiciatur. manifestum est ex inductione: quoniam omnia que sic fiunt ex substantiis fiunt.

[*As for the things that occur in an absolute fashion, some occur by transfiguration, such as a statue; others by addition, such those that grow; others by subtraction, such as Mercury carved in a stone; others by composition, such as a house; others by alteration, such as those whose matter gets modified. However, the things that occur in such manner manifestly occur from substrates.* [Aristotle] refers to natural elements as well as to artifacts when he affirms that some of the things that occur in an absolute fashion occur by transfiguration, such as a statue; others by addition, such as those that grow, for example a river swollen by various streams; others by subtraction and suppression, for example from a stone, that is to say a stone Mercury, that is to say an image of Mercury sculpted by suppressing parts of the stone; others occur by composition, such as a house; others by alteration and transfiguration, such as those things whose nature gets modified in turn, for example water which turns into air and vice versa. So that we can induce, since in every case there exists a substrate, that all things that occur in that fashion manifestly occur from substrates.][17]

However, while Roman texts leave no doubt that writing is thought of within the framework of the first approach, that of the *accessio*, for some authors, such as Francesco Lucrezi, painting is governed by the logic of *specificatio*—even if there is no mention of *nova species*—as soon as one agrees that *tabula cedit picturae* (the *tabula* appertains to the painting), because, according to him, the criterion of a higher value implies a logical qualification of painting as a *nova species*, different from the blank *tabula*.[18] Yet, according to Lucrezi, there also is the issue of the name.

Res abesse and *appellatio*

In the texts from the Justinian corpus, the creation of a new *species* is never mentioned explicitly as the reason for appurtenance of the *tabula* to the painting. In the *Institutes*, for example, the idea of the creation of a new *spe-*

cies seems to apply, first, to the transformation of one material—and only one—such as the transformation of grapes into wine, olives into oil, wool into garments, wood into a wardrobe or a seat. It concerns, therefore, the basic mutation of the form or nature of a single substance. Second, a new *species* appears when there is mixing of different materials: the *mulsum* is the product of mixing wine and honey; the *electrum* is the mixing of gold and silver. Yet, many sections of the *Digest* consider the creation of a third thing made of a support and whatever is joined to it, which, however, cannot be reduced to its two elements: the *imago*. In Book 17 of the *Quaestiones*, Papinien writes:

Si imaginem legatam heres derasit, et tabulam soluit: potest dici, actionem ex testamento durare: quia imaginis legatum non tabulae fuit.

[If the heir erased the inherited image, and if he gave (the legatee) the *tabula*, we can say the will transfer survives, because the legacy was the *imago*, and not the *tabula*.] (D.34.2.12)

And, in the seventh book *Ad edictum*, Paul writes:

Labeo et Sabinus existimant si vestimentum scissum reddatur, vel res corrupta reddita sit: veluti sciphi collisi: aut tabula rasa pictura: videri rem abesse: quoniam earum rerum pretium non in substantia sed in arte sit positum.

[Labeo and Sabinus think that if a garment is returned torn, or if a thing is returned corrupted, such as a broken vessel or a scratched painting, the thing is assumed to be absent, since the value of those things does not reside in their matter, but in the art that produced them.] (D.50.16.14)[19]

These texts are important and seem to justify one's listing of painting on the side of *specificatio*, but one should not forget that there are others who also allow viewing writing as the creation of a new *species*. A fragment by Ulpien on the subject of legacies and *fideicommis* explains what we must understand when we use the word *libri*, what the word encompasses and what objects are thus named (D.32.52).[20] This label contains all the *volumina* and *codices*, whether on papyrus, parchment, or any other support—also mentioned are linden bark, and all kinds of skins, whether animal or vegetal, as well as wax and ivory tablets. The word "books" also requires that they be entirely written (*perscripti*), but not that they be bound, sewn, glued, corrected, or adorned. One must exclude from the legacy of books all the *chartae* and *membranae* that are not written, as well as books that have been begun (*coepti*) but not finished (*perscripti*).

If one follows the issue of appellation, of what words mean, of the objects they name, one might argue that there is *specificatio* for the paintings and writing; only in the case of unfinished processes would one encounter the forms of *accessio*, or perhaps even simply an incomplete, suspended *specificatio*. It is certain, in any case, that the words *imago* and *liber* designate *species* that are not reducible to their components. But then why is *specificatio* never mentioned in the context of writings? One could answer by paraphrasing a brief gloss attributed to Rogerius (twelfth century): because in one case, one is talking about the right of specification, and in the other of the nature of the meaning of words: "Accessionis potius iure, quam ex significationis verbi natura, secundum Rog." (By virtue of the right of accession rather than by reason of the significance of the term, according to Rogerius, D.32.50.9 *Cedunt.*) Roman law seems to offer a split logic that will be reproduced by the authors of glosses and comments. Among medieval jurists, when painting and writing are envisaged as gestures connecting materials within the framework of the forms of acquisition of the *dominium*, the issue of *specificatio* is more rarely called upon than that of *accessio* where painting is concerned, and it is never specifically invoked where writing is concerned. This does not preclude that, in other contexts, particularly about legacies and the meaning of words, books and images be discussed. The debate about nomination is grounded in the relationship between *nomen* and *forma*, and addresses the meaning of words. The debate about painting and writing as acts having a bearing on rights is part of an ensemble of gestures producing effects that put *materiae* and *species* in contact to give birth to the various forms of *dominium*. When one names, one qualifies precise objects; when one speaks of *dominium*, one qualifies acts that bear on materials and things.

However, to the preceding one must add a second problem, which may account for the impossibility of assimilating *imago* and *liber*. The medieval concept of *imago* is extremely complex and incorporates realities as different to our eyes as a *tabula picta*; in the very first verses of the Bible, the second person of the Trinity, as well as man, are called "images." "Faciamus hominem ad imaginem et similitudinem nostram" (Let us make man in our image, after our likeness, Genesis 1:26), even if the *ad* of the biblical verse suggests a quest toward the restitution of a lost resemblance.[21] In the language of Boecius's logic, the *imago* "aims at representing eternal substances by visual means."[22] According to this "spiritualist" approach, *imagines* are the bodies of forms outside of matter.[23] The idea of *transitus*—that is to say the presence of the prototype in the image, typical of neoplatonic theology—was rejected during the Frankish period but asserted itself from the twelfth century on in the works of Suger and Hugues de Saint-Victor († 1141), marked by that of Pseudo-Dionysius the Areopagite, elaborated in the fifth century and whose impact on the West remained limited, despite Jean Scot Erigène's translation and commentaries.[24] Pseudo-Dionysius's approach offers to rehabilitate matter, particularly materials that exalt light, such as gold or stones, as a sign of spirituality, which will dominate the last part of the Middle Ages. During the Justinian period and through the age of the gloss and commentary writers, this presence of the immaterial prototype in the *imago* endows it with an existence that cannot be derived solely from the union of materials. This way of approaching the *imago* is not dominant among jurists of the *tabula picta*; still, it can explain why *imago* and *liber* cannot be thought of under the same logic.

We now have to return to the themes of *accessio* and *specificatio*. It is beyond my competence to rule on the status of painting and writing during the classical and postclassical Roman law period; however, I would like to offer some thoughts on the relationship between *accessio*, *specificatio*, and painting or writing in the works of gloss and commentary writers. I will start with *accessio*, as it is argued more often. But first we must address a problem of terminology.

Charta, *membrana*, and *tabula*

When gloss and commentary writers use the word *charta*, one should not believe they are systematically referring to the papyrus, which is the original meaning of the word. The word *charta* is a transliteration of the Greek word that, from the fifth century onward, designates the sheets, the elements of the scroll. However, even in Byzantium, it would have been legitimate to translate *charta* as "paper" to the extent that the word designates "material to be written made of strips of papyrus," as well as, generally, a support for writing, as neutral, in any case, as paper in English. Besides, paper, used in Byzantium from the eighth century on, will make the word *charta* drift from "papyrus" to "paper," even if paper manuscripts are identified by their origin, for example *charta Damascena*, "paper from Damascus."[25] *Charta* is often used in the West to designate generally the support for writing, parchment, then paper from the second half of the eighth century—on very rare occasions, by metonymy, that word has been used to mean "book."[26] Papyrus was known, nonetheless, and used in the West as the support for writing during the first millennium A.D. and even beyond, since the original bulls still in existence evidence its use by the papal chancellery until the middle of the eleventh century, and that type of support could also be named *charta juncea* or *charta papyri*. The phrase *charta juncea* appears in a text by King Ottokar of Bohemia from 1224 confirming a bull by John XV for the monastery of Margaret of Prague. When Peter the Venerable enumerates the various writing supports used in his time, he recalls those made "ex juncis orientalium paludum" (with the stems of Oriental reeds).[27] As to *charta papyri*, an act of Frederic II's from 1231 is the oldest known example.

The word *membrana*, also used by gloss and commentary writers, is used more specifically and generally designates parchment.[28]

A third, more rare word appears in the ordinary glosses: *bombicina*, derived from the noun *bombix* or *bambix* which, in medieval Latin, designated cotton.[29]

However, usage of the word *tabula* in legal texts is rather particular. It is always used where painting is concerned, never about writing, and can be construed both literally, as a wooden board, and more generically, as the support for a painting. But the words *tabula*, *tabella*, or *tabellula* are used extremely often to designate writing supports. In fact, the use of writing tablets was quite common in the Roman and medieval worlds, and even at the beginning of the modern era.[30] Baudri de Bourgueil (ca. 1045–1130) dedicates two poems in their entirety to such tablets, one being *Ludendo de tabulis*, and the other, a graver one, *Ad tabulas*.[31] The importance of tablets, and particularly of wax tablets, as a writing support in Western culture allows Richard and Mary Rouse to speak of a "wax tablet culture."[32] Nonetheless, the word *tabula* is used by the jurists exclusively in connection with painting.

Chapter 2
Accessio

Two of the most interesting texts about *accessio* are Placentin's *Summa* to the *Institutes*, probably written during the last third of the twelfth century,[1] and Azo's *Summa,*[2] written at the beginning of the thirteenth century. In fact, Placentin is the first to discuss the *tabula picta* at length within an original system. According to him, the *ius gentium* governs two modes of acquisition of the *dominium*: "Per apprehensionem et per accessionem" (by appropriation and by accession). The first mode itself breaks down into four subcategories: *captio* (taking), *permutatio* (exchange), *traditio* (delivery), and *occupatio* (occupation). The one that concerns us, *accessio*, breaks down into two types: *discretam* (separate) and *continuam* (continuous, in a spatial sense); this first category always implies the idea of birth; and this is where Placentin will classify painting, whereas writing, on the contrary, will find its place in the *accessio continua*.

The *accessio discreta* designates the young of an animal which, if owned by me, appertain to my estate, just like a child born of my slave, the new *species* born from matter, the island born of the sea (this example is split between the birth of the island that emerges from the water and the moment it actually becomes someone's property, which obeys the principle of occupation), and the island born of a river, which, being in the middle, will belong to the residents of both banks, or to those of the nearest bank. The idea of birth does not necessarily imply the idea of nature, because the *species* in question are man-made. The animals, the persons, the islands, the *species*, among which painting belongs under certain conditions, are born, and are born separately. However, there exists another distinction, which divides this category into two. Within the *accessio discreta*, there is the *accessio* that happens "de re ad personas," and the one which happens "de re ad rem."

Acquiritur autem duobus modis per discretam scilicet accessionem, et per continuam. Per discretam alias de re ad personam, alias de re ad rem. De re ad personas puta ubi ex animalibus nostris foetus, uel ex ancillis nostris partus nascitur. Idem si insula quae in mare nascitur. Idem in specificatione per operam [. . .] De re ad rem discreta

fit accessio, ut si insula nascatur in flumine, nata enim in medio praeter omnem oc-
cupationem fit utrorumque possidentium. Si uero sit proximior alteri ripae, eorum
fiet tantum, qui possident, eatenus tamen, quatenus insula cum nascitur frontem agri
cuiusque respicit.

[There exist two modes of acquisition by accession: separate accession, and continuous
accession. Separate accession can be found sometimes from a thing to a person, sometimes from one thing to another. There is accession from a thing to a person for example
when young are born of one of our cattle, or a child of one of our servants; the same
goes when an island is born from the sea. Similarly in cases of specification. (. . .) There
is accession from one thing to another if, for example, an island happens to be born in a
river: if born in the middle, free of any occupant, it belongs to the owners of both banks.
But, if it is closer to one bank, it will belong solely to the owners of that bank, to the
extent, however, that upon its birth, the island was facing their lands.] (p. 22)[3]

The last category contains one example only: that of the island born of a river,
which appertains to the riverbank owner as if, once born, it merely extended
the limits of one thing—the riverbank owner's domain—without retaining
its original autonomy. The "accessio discreta de re ad personas," on the contrary, gives birth to a thing that is not of the order of an extension, but rather
of the production into existence of a thing which, individual in perpetuity,
appertains to someone's patrimony.

For Placentin, *specificatio* is a form of *accessio*, of that "accessio discreta
de re ad personas" which results from the birth of a separate and legally distinct thing that appertains to the patrimony of a person. Thus, for him, painting belongs to *specificatio* under certain conditions only: the quality of the
pigments and the subject of the representation. If those conditions are satis-
fied, then the *imago* is born, as animals, men, and islands are born; it is a new
thing, previously without existence, that must belong to the painter, that is to
say he who created it, he who gave it birth.

On the contrary, the *accessio continua* designates that which, without a
birth, becomes added to someone's estate; in this case, it is always an *accessio* "de re ad rem." Thus, the *crusta* that water bring to my land, the drifting
trees the river carries and which root on my property,[4] things joined by *ferruminatio*, and generally all that belongs to the category of *alluvio*: that is to
say, *incrementum latens* and *incrementum apparens*. The *incrementum latens*
(imperceptible) concerns what is brought onto my field by the river, provided
the adjunction happens little by little:

Acquiritur per accessionem continuam, ut si flumen in fundum tuum de alieno crus-
tam intulerit, ita tamen si iam unitatem cum tuo fecerit, quod ex eo apparebit si ar-

bores quas traxerat, ibi iam radices egerint [...] Per alluuionem quoque, quod est incrementum latens, acquiritur sicut per incrustationem.

[There is acquisition by continuous accession, for example, if a river brings into your domain a deposit of soil coming from the domain of another, provided however that this deposit becomes one with your domain: that will be clear if trees carried by the river have already rooted in it. (...) There is also acquisition by alluvium, which designates an imperceptible increase by deposit of alluvia] (p. 22)[5]

To explain the *alluvio* understood as *incrementum latens*, Azo will evoke the growth of fruit, which renders the idea expressed in the *Institutes* by which *alluvio* implies the slow adjunction, defined as an imperceptible process. The text of I.2.1.20 states:

Praeterea quod per alluuionem agro tuo flumen adiicit, iure gentium tibi acquiritur. Est autem alluuio incrementum latens. Per alluuione autem id adiici videtur, quod ita paulatim adiicitur, vt intelligi non possit, quantum quoquo momento temporis adiiciatur.

[Besides, what the river adds to the lands by alluvium belongs to you under the *ius gentium*. The alluvium designates an imperceptible increase: one regards as an adjunction by alluvium any imperceptible adjunction to the point that neither its quantity nor its timing can be perceived.]

In his *Summa*, Azo explains:

Nam et si tota die figas intuitum imbecillitas uisus tam subtilia incrementa perpendere non potest; ut in cucurbita.

[In fact, even if one stares all day, the feebleness of eyesight does not permit to measure increases as minute as those of a squash.][6]

To this, one should contrast the *incrementum apparens* (visible, apparent): if the power of the river tears away part of your land and pushes it toward the neighboring land, it remains yours as long as trees do not attach it thereto by their roots.

However, it is the verb *cedere*, and not *accedere*, which is used most often by Placentin to qualify the relationship between things that are (although this is not the vocabulary he uses), in the final analysis, united by man's hand, without birth, and without the river's flow. The *cessio* includes the relationship between the construction timber and the house, gold, silver, pearls and gems, purple and canvas, buildings and their land, things planted and sowed, writing and *charta*, as well as painting when it has not produced a new *species*, and to the extent it is governed by the principle of *ferruminatio*, which posits the theoretical impossibility of separating united things.

Ergo hoc uerbum cedit aliter accipitur in tigno, sicut expositum est, aliter in ferruminato siue depicto, aliter in sato, plantato.

[That verb *cedit* (it appertains to) thus has different meanings, as we explained, whether one speaks of construction timber, of an object welded by *ferruminatio*, or of a painted object, of a sowed vegetable, of a planted vegetable.] (p. 23)

Writing, in particular, is governed, like buildings, plants, or grains, by the principle *superficies solo cedit* (the surface appertains to the land). Finally, a double category designates the union of things that are liquid, capable of being fused or mixed: *confusio* and *commixtio*. They are not relevant to the theme of the *tabula picta*, but we will examine them later in order to distinguish them from other modes of union of materials, which, on the contrary, *are* relevant to it.

As for Azo, after dealing with occupation, the model of which is the catching of wild beasts, birds, and fish, he addresses the problem of *accessio*. There is what is acquired "per accessionem discreta, uel secretam," or what is governed by *accessio* "concretam seu continuam." If one considers that *secreta* and *discreta* are synonymous, as are *concreta* and *continua*, one again encounters the opposition proposed by Placentin between separate and continuous *accessio*. The next section of the text seems to suggest this.

Nam quae ex animalibus dominio tuo subiectis nata sunt, tibi acquiruntur [...] Preaterea, quod per alluvionem agro tuo flumen adiicit, iure gentium tibi acquiritur.

[Indeed, the small animals depending on your property belong to you. (. . .) Besides, what the river adds to your lands by alluvium belongs to you according to the *ius gentium*.] (Ibid., *ad* 30)[7]

In truth, there exist numerous differences between Placentin's and Azo's classifications. Two are of particular interest to us.

First, contrary to what Placentin stated, *accessio* does not subsume *specificatio*, and neither painting nor writing come under that last category. About *tabula picta*, only *accessio* is discussed. Second, birth as a criterion permitting the regrouping of the progeny of animals and slaves, islands, and all new *spe-*

cies does not exist in Azo's work; the *accessio discreta* concerns progeny only, and this will be carried over into the ordinary gloss. However, more generally, it is the very structure of the classification that changes because the most important criterion for Azo is that of the agent of *accessio*. Placentin did not reason thus but one realizes, while reading Azo, that his interpretation may coincide in parts with that of the master from Montpellier. In fact, Placentin took into account an ensemble of phenomena that implied either a superhuman power or the idea of birth; and that ensemble, about which he always uses the verb *accedere*, is contrasted to the one constituted around the verb *cedere*, which applies to a human action not leading to a birth.

However, Azo resorts to another category that was not used by the Romans either: "divina natura tantum operante" *accessio*. Progeny, and things brought by water, are governed by divine acts exclusively. This is the first term of a classification of *accessio* made up of three categories: the *accessio* caused by "diuina natura tantum operante" (only through acts of divine nature), that which is caused by "humana natura tamen operante" (through the acts of human nature), and the "accessio divina et natura et humana cooperante" (the accession due to the joint acts of divine nature and human nature). The accession that depends on human acts concerns the adjunction by *adpumbatio* and *ferruminatio*, building, as well as painting and writing.[8] Azo affirms that this category is also applicable to "intextis uel insertis uel inclusis" (things incorporated to fabric, set in, or inlaid), such as purple added to a garment. Finally, the *accessio* whose agents are both God and man concerns plants in the ground and sowed grain, that is, all that is discussed starting at I.2.1.35: "cultura et cura," as well as trees that root in a neighbor's field, with the caveat that if plants or grains fall randomly on a land with which they become one, without man's intervention, then one is back at the first form of *accessio*, that which derives from divine acts.[9]

No subordinate classification seems to govern the fate of divine accessions: neither the part and the whole, nor value, nor ornament can be a second criterion in determining those things' destiny. Only God can withhold what he gave by *accessio*, by making the waters cover the land that their receding had given me or by carrying away my trees or chunks of land detached by water toward the riverbank of another. As for human acts as principle of *accessio*, they seem divided into a value-based logic, which governs painting and writing—Azo claims with force that writing should be assimilated to painting—and a principle of accessoriness, which may lead to opposite readings; since purple could be regarded as changing nothing in a finished garment, thus being a mere accessory to it, one could assert that it becomes part of the garment if it is added in order to be conserved.[10]

For Azo, the *specificatio* plays no part as a criterion to assess painting or writing. It designates the processes for making wine, oil, *mulsum*, plaster and collyrium, wool garments, boats, and wardrobes and seats made out of wooden boards, to which he applies the *media sententia*. Painting and writing must be thought of within the terms of "accessio per humane nature solicitudinem" (accession due to application of a human nature). It is this principle of the agent only that distinguishes the drifting trees from progeny or sowed grains.

However, something else is important in his *Summa*. Indeed, Azo was the first to develop what Martino[11] had been the first to suggest: the exaltation of the art of writing and its assimilation to the value-based principle governing painting. How should the difference between painting and writing in the *Institutes* be explained, Azo asks.

Queritur, cur aliud sit in scriptis, quam in pictis? respondeo, quia olim fere semper erat pretiosior charta, quam scriptura: et e converso pictura erat pretiosior tabula. vnde tabula cedebat picturae [...] Vel quod ibi dicitur, referendum est ad scripturam, et ad chartam. Hodie autem scriptores nostri temporis facti sunt pictores, et fere semper inuenitur pretiosior scriptura, quam charta. Vnde propter alteratum cursus nature, vel consuetudinis, posset hodie contrarium responderi.

[Question: why are writings and paintings treated differently? Answer: because in the old days the *charta* was almost always more precious than the writing; painting, on the contrary, was more precious than the tablet. So the tablet would appertain to the painting. (...) And one must apply this observation to the writing and the *charta*: the scribes of today have become painters, and one almost always observes that writing is more precious than the *charta*. Thus, due to the changes that occurred in the course of nature and in usage, one could answer the opposite today.] (Azo, *Summa, ad* 42)

Thus it is the value that governs painting and writing; however, it does so within the context of *accessio*—and he makes fun of Placentin who had tried to explain painting within the context of the *specificatio* by assessing the subject of the representation and the quality of the pigments:

P. qui ait locum habere quod dicit lex, tabulam picturae cedere; ita demum si pingatur homo non vrsus: et ita si pictura sit de bonis coloribus, non de calce, uel encausto. et alia multa fabulatus est de pictura.

[According to Placentin, the law would stipulate that the tablet appertains to the painting if, and only if, the painting represents a man and not a bear, in colors of good quality, and not in lime or ink. And he adds a thousand other fables about painting.]

This assimilation of writing to the principles governing painting corresponds to a new perception of writing. The rare surviving testimonials from the late Middle Ages that reflect on writing practices seem to indicate that purely physical writing activity, such as the drawing of the letters and the graphic layout of the copied texts, came second after allegorical significance. In the middle of the tenth century, chronicle writer Eckhard I of Saint-Gall used monks who were the least gifted for studying for manuscript copying: "et quos ad literarum studia tardiores vidisset, ad scribendum occupaverat et lineandum" (and those in whom he had noticed a lesser vivacity in the study of the texts, he had used for writing and illuminating).[12] However, from the thirteenth century on, calligraphy becomes an art, an end in itself, and spreads beyond the monasteries. *De Laude scriptorum* of John Gerson and Johannes Trithemius indeed seem meant primarily to exalt and almost encourage the virtues of the practice of copying in monasteries.[13] Writing masters and professional scribes appear.[14] The material features of writing are called "manual orthography." Thus, the author of the *Tractatus* from the Abbey of Kremsmünster (fifteenth century) states:

Ortographia est duplex, una docens litterarum et sillabarum quantitates [...] Alia est ars scribendi et ortographia manualis et est scientia docens recte scribere id est litteras et sillabas [...] debite protrahere et ornare per regulas unam alteri combinare et dicitur ab orthos quod est rectum et graphos scriptura.

[There are two orthographies: one teaches the quantity of letters and syllables (...); the other designates the art of writing, manual orthography, and it is a science that teaches proper writing, that is, how to trace the letters and syllables correctly, embellish them according to the rules, and link one letter to the next. The word comes from *orthos*, "by the rule," and *graphos*, "writing."]

Of all the mechanical arts, he adds, it is the best, the most dignified, and the noblest "quia omnibus aliis spiritualior et opere subtilior, fine ultimo videlicet ipsi Deo glorioso appropinquat" (since it is a more spiritual and a more delicate craft than all the others because of its ultimate goal, [the art of writing] evidently is akin to the God of glory Himself, ibid., p. 253). This type of treatise describes the lines composing each letter, their thickness, blank spaces, proportions, the manner, in sum, of tracing each letter according to its "proprietates substanciales."

However, the greatest praise of the art of writing is to be found in a late treatise, written around 1468 by Gabriel Altadell, notary and copyist in the service of the Neapolitan court of Alfonso V the Magnificent.[15] It is different from previous works in that the author does not describe the manner of drawing each letter but discusses at length the *moderamem*, that is, the preparation of the pen, the movements of the hand, the look of the entire page, and the different types of writing. Before reverting to the humility that befits any practice that dispenses with implorations to God, the treatise, destined for his disciple Ludovicus, states that

Ipse enim ars tantam celsitudinem in se continet, ut nullus inter omnes scriptores constiterint qui partem etiam minimam perfecto adeptus sit; in qua si quis ita excellens reperiatur, ut inter omnes principatum obtineat, id monstri simile est, imo magis divinum quam humanum.

[In effect, in the art itself resides such high nobility that, among all the scribes that existed, none mastered its perfection, even in an infinitely small part; if one met a man who excelled in this art to the point of having absolute preeminence, that would amount to a prodigy, better, it would be divine rather than human.] (Ibid., p. 258)

Besides, until the twelfth century, signed manuscripts are few in number and often correspond to works in which the copyist is also the illuminator; however after that date the subscriptions allow the "pure" copyists to be identified.[16] From the thirteenth century, the percentage of those who sign their work increases. This is how Carla Bozzolo and Ezio Ornato were able to establish, from a series of French collections, that the rate of dated manuscripts is, in the fifteenth century, "approximately 2.5 times superior to that of the 14th century, and 7.5 times superior to that of the 13th century"[17] (dating implies the presence of a colophon providing information about the scribe and the patron, who, besides, may be the same person). If, in the monastic *scriptoria*, writing in the service of God commands the respect of anonymity, the frequency of signing in the last centuries of the Middle Ages assumes a publicity function for the growing number of professional copyists.[18]

The metaphor that makes writing a painting, that justifies for jurists a new perception of the practices and price of writings, appears also in other texts. In the eleventh century, for example, the word *depingere* can designate the act of writing; and in the twelfth century Adelard of Bath speaks of writing as a "painting on parchment."[19] Later, after the propedeutics of drawing became widely accepted among painters, Pier Paolo Vergerio (a humanist and canonist born in Capodistria in 1370, tutor of the princes of Carrara in Padua, secretary to popes Innocent VII and Gregory XII, in the service of emperor Sigismund until his death in 1440) will compare it to writing.[20] Drawing, he states, "does not in practice pass as a liberal study except so far as it relates to the writing of characters—writing being the same thing as portraying" (designativa vero nunc in usu non est pro liberali, nisi quantum forsitan ad scripturam attinet—scribere namque it ipsum est protrahere atque designare).[21] The relationship between painting and writing is even inverted by Alberti in a passage which, according to Michael Baxandall, is "not entirely without malice,"[22] where he exhorts beginners in the art of painting to do what is observed by those who teach writing. "They first teach separately all the characters of the elements, then teach how to compose syllables, then, finally, expressions. Our beginners should follow this method when they paint."[23] The comparison takes place at a very elementary stage of the painter's training and we know that Alberti's model is not calligraphic practice, but humanist rhetoric. The analogy, however, speaks eloquently to the new dignity of writing.

Two centuries after Azo, Paolo da Castro (ca. 1360–1441, a pupil of Baldus's in Perugia, author of commentaries and *consilia*, professor in several universities), profoundly influenced by the vocabulary of scholastics, proposes a new division of *accessio* into four categories, which rests upon the relationship between the whole and the part.

De quadruplici accessione. Primo quando res mea tanquam pars accedit tuae tanquam toti particulari [...]. i. sicut est statua, vel scyphus, et in hoc distinguitur, an accedat per ferruminationem quia si per eandem materiam an per applumbaturam, quia fit per diuersam, vt primo casu desinam esse dominus nec possum eam vendicare etiam postquam fuerit separata [...] Secundo loquitur, quando res mea accedit tuae tanquam toti vniuersali, ut ouis mea gregi tuo, que cum non mutet speciem, non desinit esse mea, et semper uendicare possum [...] Tertio cum accedit tuae tanquam toti integrali, ut tignum meum domui tuae, quo casu non desino esse dominus [...] Quarto quando accedit tuae, quod non potest dici totum, sed est talis sine qua res mea stare non potest, puta, cum de caementis meis aedificatur domus in solo tuo, sine quo solo non potest domus consistere, non tamen dicitur totum, sed pars domus [...] Potest etiam poni exemplum, de litera mea facta in charta tua, sine qua litera mea stare non potest, uel de pictura mea facta in tabula tua. [...] breuiter dic, quod interdum pictura fit ad ornatum tabulae, et ipsius tabulae gratia, ut in cameris dominorum, ubi pinguntur postes de uili materia ad ipsorum ornatum, et tunc pictura cedit tabulae [...] aut econtra, tabula adiicitur gratia picturae, et tunc aut est uilis pictura, et idem dici potest [...]. Aut est pretiosa, et tunc econtra, tabula cedit picturae, ut in contrario, et quae fit ratio differentiae inter picturam, et scripturam. dic, ut ibi notatur.

[The four forms of accession. The first form is found when my property appertains to your property insofar as it is a part of a particular whole (...) for example a statue or a vase; and in this case, one distinguishes between accession by *ferruminatio*—welding by means of a substance identical to that of the parts—and accession by *applumbatura*—welding by means of a different substance: in the first case, I cease being the owner of the property and I have no way of claiming it, even after separation. (. . .) We encounter the second form when my property appertains to yours as to a universal whole, for example when my ewe appertains to your flock: since it does not change *species*, it never ceases belonging to me and I retain the ability to reclaim it (. . .). The third form is that where my property appertains to yours as to an integral whole, thus my construction timber to your house: in which case I do not cease owning it.[24] (. . .) The fourth is encountered when (my thing) appertains to yours, which cannot be called a whole, but is such that my thing would not continue to exist without it, for example, a house built in sandstone on your land cannot continue to exist without that land; yet, one does not speak of it as a whole, but as part of the house. (. . .) One can also mention the example of the letter written on your *charta*, without which the letter cannot survive, or that of the painting I draw on your board. (. . .) You must say in a few words that the painting is made to embellish a tablet, to the benefit of the tablet only, as in noblemen's rooms, where the door jambs are painted with a valueless material to embellish them: the painting then appertains to the tablet (. . .) or on the contrary, the tablet is added for the benefit of the painting, and then it is one of two things: either the painting is of little value and one can say as here [the painting appertains to the tablet] or the painting is precious, and then it is the opposite: the support appertains to the painting, because one is in the reverse situation. Here is the reason for the difference that separates painting and writing. You must rule according to these directions.][25]

So that, in the final analysis, if the principle does apply to writing, it is annulled as to painting, which is governed either by the *ornandi causa*—that is, by determining which, the painting or the support, is adorning the other—or by the criterion of value.

   The *accessio* thus has multiple meanings; it plays a part in variable architectures and causes painting and writing to be included in a series of extraordinary diversity due to what they include as well as to what they exclude. Still, the number of judicial solutions is not infinite. In fact, Placentin's, Azo's, and Paolo da Castro's classifications, which were organized more than two centuries apart according to different criteria (birth or adjunction, agent, or part and whole), lead to answers that were already present in the Justinian text. For Placentin, writing is incorporated to the *charta*—but painting is not incorporated to the *tabula*—provided it produce new *species*, which hinges on the quality and subject of the representation. For Azo, writing and painting are of a greater price and, most of the time, subordinate their supports. For Paolo da Castro, as in the Justinian text, that same price criterion distinguishes a valueless writing from a precious painting. However, even though solutions vary little, their justifications proliferate.

Chapter 3
Specificatio

The first gloss writer who thought of painting within the explicit framework of *specificatio* is Placentin, writing about the *Institutes*. However, one should not forget that, for him, *specificatio* was a category subsumed into *accessio*, and most particularly into "accessio discreta de re ad personam," which ranked *specificatio* on a par with the progeny of animals and slaves and with the islands born of the sea. Placentin incarnates a defense of art and technique that is not often present in the debate.

Envisaged within the framework of the rules of *accessio*, painting characteristically inverts the principle by which things that exist regardless of their support dominate, for, on the contrary, painting absorbs its support (conversely, the principle of *superficies solo cedit* governs writing, to the extent that writing gets incorporated into the parchment). However, if envisaged under the logic of that particular form of *accessio* that is Placentin's *specificatio*, painting must be ruled by the *media sententia*, that is, according to a logic of irreducibility of the raw material in its original state, which allocates ownership of the *icona* or *imago* to the painter, as *specificanti*: "Sed nobis media sententia placuit; ergo pictor, cum dominus sit picturae, directo poterit iconam ab omni possessore vindicare" (But we favor the intermediary opinion; the painter, as he is the owner of his painting, will be able to propose a *rei vindicatia directa* [the owner's typical act]).["]1 Those two terms, *icona* and *imago*, used by Placentin to designate the *tabula picta*, do not appear in the text of the *quaestio*, but *imago* is used in the D.50.16.13 and 14. Placentin envisages the value of a painting in terms of *dignitas*; and it necessarily partakes in the creation of a new *species*, but under certain conditions. Before conceding that painting produces a new *species*, it is necessary to evaluate its subject, the materials used, and probably the technical skills used in its making. The *dignitas* is the condition of *specificatio*.

For Placentin, the union of colors to a surface has not in and of itself the power to produce a new *species*. Only the *dignitas* of the subject represented, the quality of the colors, and the careful crafting of the finished work can lead to the existence of a radically new thing, irreducible to the sum of its parts. Placentin's arguments will be endorsed by Odofredo, who emphasizes the subject of the representation, and these arguments bring the word *dignitas* closer to one of the meanings proposed by Du Cange: *Dignitas* "idem quod Majestas, imago et effigies alicujus Sancti" (*Dignitas* has the same meaning as *Majestas*; it designates the image and the representation of a Saint).[2] Nonetheless, it is true that, even if there is no new *species*, the painter must retain the *icona*, not by right of *specificatio*, but because it is impossible to separate the painting from its support without destroying it.

Scripta, licet sint aurea, cedunt chartae [. . .] Si quis in aliena tabula pinxerit, quidam dicunt picturam tabulae cedere, sicut litera chartae (quia nec litera sine charta, nec pictura sine tabula esse potest) alii putauerunt semper picturae tabulam cedere, propter dignitatem picturae [. . .] In summa notandum est: cum sit pictura non fieri speciem; ergo licet possit abrasa redire in tabulam, non tamen icona domini tabulae sed pictoris fiet; maxime: cum id sine laesione fieri non possit; vel si concedatur factam esse speciem, dicatur in pictura speciale: meo iuditio, pictura hic intelligitur, si quis depinxerit hominem non ursum uel leonem. Item; meo iuditio, ita intelligatur, si pictura non de calce uel encausto conficiatur, sed de coloribus uariis confectis depingatur.

[The writings, be they in gold, appertain to the *charta* . . . If someone painted on someone else's board, some say the painting appertains to the board, just as the letters appertain to the *charta* (because the letters cannot survive without the *charta*, nor the painting without the board); others think the board always appertains to the painting by reason of the dignity of the painting . . . In sum, one must note the following: even though a painting is at issue, there is no new *species*; thus, even though the scraped board may become a board again, the icon must belong to the painter, and not to the owner of the board, all the more so that it cannot be done without damage; but if we admitted that a new *species* was produced, we would say so about a particular painting, and to my mind, we mean by painting the fact that one painted a man, and not a bear or a lion. Also, in my opinion, one would understand it thus: if the painting was not made in lime or ink, but, on the contrary, was painted in various man-made colors.][3]

Therefore for Placentin the "birth" of a painting conceived of as a new *species* is a function of two criteria: the subject of the representation, the exclusion of certain substances, such as *calce* (lime) and *incausto* (ink) and the exhibition of "coloribus variis confectis." I would like to pause on this issue. Inks are generally designated by the words *incaustum* and *atramentum* (much rarer in legal texts). Originally, *atramentum* designated black inks (from *ater*); and *incaustum* designated purple ink reserved for the emperors. However, both terms became synonymous in medieval times.[4] Here, the master from Montpellier seems to evoke the practice of an art, the use of techniques that are knowable, not only through the analysis of the objects themselves, but also through existing treatises.

The *De diversis artibus*, written by the Benedictine monk Theophilus, may have been written in an important hub of the arts in northwestern Germany in the first half of the twelfth century, the author of which, writing under a pseudonym, could be Roger of Helmarshausen. Helmarshausen had grown under imperial patronage and, in the twelfth century, became one of the most important centers for the arts in northwestern Germany, receiving commissions from bishops such as Henry of Werl and princes such as Henry the Lion.[5] Theophilus describes not only the preparation of the colors but also the various stages of the painting, and he is the first one to describe a true "technique of representation."[6] Here are some excerpts:

De temperamentum colorum in nudis corporibus. Color qui dicitur membrana, quo pinguntur facies et nuda corpora, sic componitur. Tolle cerosam, id est album, quod fit ex plumbo, et mitte eam, non tritam sed ita ut est siccam, in uas cupreum uel ferreum, et pone super prunas ardentes et combure, donec conuertatur in flauum colorem. Deinde tere eum et admisce ei albam cerosam et cenobrium, donec carni similis fiat. Quorum colorum mixtura in tuo sit arbitrio, ut si uerbi gratia rubeas facies habere uis, plus adde cenobrii; si uero candidas, plus appone albi; si autem pallidas, appone pro cenobrio modicum prasini.

[Recipe of colors for naked bodies. The color named *membrana*, used to paint faces and disrobed bodies, is prepared as follows. Take ceruse, that is, white made with lead, deposit it, not as a powder but dry, in a copper or iron vessel, put it on burning embers and leave it on the fire until it turns golden. Then reduce it to powder and incorporate into it white ceruse and cinnabar, until you obtain a tint similar to that of flesh. The mixing of these colors must be left to your personal judgment: if, for example, you want rubicund faces, add more cinnabar; if, on the contrary, you want them brighter, put more white; but if you want them pale, substitute a little green to the cinnabar.] (p. 5)

De posc primo. Cum uero membranam miscueris et inde facies et nuda corpora impleueris, admisce ei prasinum et rubeum, qui comburitur ex ocra, et modicum cenobrii, et confice posc; ex quo designabis supercilia et oculos, nares et os, mentum et fossulas circa nares et timpora, rugas in fronte et collo et rotunditatem faciei, barbas iuuenum et articulos manuum et pedum et omnia membra qua distinguuntur in nudo corpore.

[The first *posc*. And after having mixed the *membrana*, and then coated the faces and disrobed bodies, incorporate into it some green, some red from burnt ocher, and a little cinnabar, to prepare the *posc*. You will use it to draw the eyebrows and the eyes, the nose and the mouth, the chin and the lightly hollow areas of the nose and temples, the wrinkles on the forehead and neck, the oval of the face, the beard of young men, the finger and toe joints, as well as all visible parts of a naked body.] (pp. 5–6)

De lvmina prima. Post haec misce cum simplici membrana cerosam tritam, et compone colorem qui dicitur lumina, unde illuminabis supercilia, nasum in longitudine.

[The first touch of light. After that, mix powdered ceruse with pure *membrana* and prepare the color known as *lumina*, which will allow you to lighten up the eyebrows and the ridge of the nose.] (pp. 6–7)

De veneda in oculis ponenda. Deinde commisce nigrum cum modico albo, qui color uocatur ueneda, et inde imple pupillas oculorum.

[The application of the *veneda* on the eyes. Then mix some black with a little white— this is the color called *veneda*—then color the pupil of the eyes.] (p. 7)

De posc secvndo. Postea accipe posc, de quo supra dictum est, et admisce ei amplius de prasino et rubeo, ita ut umbra sit anterioris coloris, et imple medium spatium inter supercilia et oculos et sub oculis medium et iuxta nasum et inter os et mentum et granos seu barbulas adolescentum et palmas dimidias uersus pollicem et pedes supra minores articulos et facies puerorum et mulierum a mento usque ad timpora.

[The second *posc*. After that, take the *posc* discussed above, incorporate more green and red into it, so as to turn it into the shadow of the previous color, and color the spaces between the eyebrows and the eyes, under the eyes, close to the nose, and between the mouth and the chin. Also color the pigtails and the fuzz of adolescents, the half of the palm on the side of the thumb, the feet at the level of the phalanxes, as well as the faces of children and women from the chin to the temples.]

The treatise emphasizes, not only what Placentin and Odofredo after him will assume as technical competence when they evoke varied man-made colors, but also the centrality of the human figure. As for the lime Placentin mentions, it is used in preparations such as glue (*glutine casei*) as well as in the elaboration of the colors, and most particularly those to be used for murals, which must adhere to the wall when they dry:

De mixtura uestimentorum in mvro ... Cum imagines uel aliarum rerum effigies pertrahuntur in muro sicco, statim aspergatur aqua tamdiu, donec omnino madidus sit. Et in eodem humore liniantur omnes colores qui superponendi sunt, qui omnes calce misceantur et cum ipso muro siccentur, ut haereant.

[The composition of wall ornaments ... When one draws human figures or other shapes on a dry wall, one must immediately spray water until the wall is entirely damp. And one must spread all the colors to be applied directly on the damp surface, so that they all mix with the lime and dry at the same time as the wall, so as to adhere to it.] (p. 13)

However, it does not appear as a substance used on its own. As for ink, it seems to refer to drawing—which it is still called *pictura*—rather than painting, which must be made with carefully prepared colors. Drawings, which are not considered as finished works until the Renaissance, lack the autonomy necessary to fit within *specificatio*.[7]

Cennino Cennini, who regards painting on *tabula* as "the most agreeable and most proper art there is in our profession" ("la più dolce arte e la più netta che abbino nell'arte nostra"),[8] describes the various stages of the work with even greater minutiae in his treatise written between the end of the fourteenth century and the beginning of the fifteenth century in the Veneto region. First, one uses a mixture of glue and sawdust to fill the holes and imperfections in the surface; one then applies two layers of glue prepared with shreds of parchment according to a recipe previously given. After having scraped the surface—an operation repeated after each step—one applies a thick mix of plaster and glue, followed by several layers (at least eight on flat surfaces) of thin plaster, with less glue than in the previous application. Once the surface is ready, one draws first with willow charcoal, and then with diluted ink.[9] The treatise then discusses gilding, which Cennini particularly liked.

This text, as well as that of Theophilus, allows us to understand the idea expressed by Placentin and, as we shall see, Odofredo after him, according to which *specificatio* happens only at the end of multiple and successive operations, which carefully prepare the support before the drawing, before the application of a layer of gold, and before the application of layers of color which will define the features on the *membrana*. Not every *pictura* implies the birth of a new thing. Only the finished, perfected work representing God, the Virgin, or at least human figures, can claim to be "born."

Odofredo is, to my knowledge, the only one to repeat the arguments of the master from Montpellier, amplifying them not without wit. In order for the *tabula* to appertain to the painting, one must, he says, have painted the *figura* of our lord Jesus Christ, of the Holy Virgin, of the apostles, or of a man, and not a bear, or the slugs the French paint to mock the Italians, or yet those drawings drawn by the Italians, representing a man crushing spices or preparing green sauce;[10] this derisive painting was not foreign to a specifically

Italian and very widespread practice between the thirteenth and the fifteenth centuries, that of slanderous painting which was a form of judicial sentence.[11] One must also have employed better colors, and not charcoal, ink, *gypso lunacarii*,[12] or *alio vilissimo colore*, because painting is *pretiosa ratione forme vel conditionis*.

Thus, when the gloss and comment writers repeat Placentin's opinion by referring to the *pretiositas* understood solely as the value, they cancel the distinction between various forms of value, since it is not only the *pretium*, but also the *dignitas* which governs the logic of *specificatio*, and which justifies the distinction between painting and writing. If only the *pretium* in its pecuniary sense were considered, then the principle could simply be reversed, says Placentin about the Justinian text, and the high price of a *tabula* would attract that of a cheaper painting; but it is not so: "non debet magni pretii tabula trahere ad se viliorem picturam" (a tablet carrying a high price must not attract to itself a painting of lesser value).[13] The *dignitas* rests on what is represented and on abidance to the rules of the art. Azo will make fun of this unusual position by writing about Placentin's "fabulations."

The criterion of *specificatio* appears in a long gloss Paola Maffei attributes to Jean Bassian (✝ ca. 1193), who equates it to *ferruminatio*—the uniting of two things by way of an identical matter, such as for example the uniting of two gold pieces joined together by gold—and also to *plantatio* and *satio*. He contrasts this series to that of things united by *adplumbatio*—the uniting of two things or matters by way of a different matter, such as for example the uniting of two gold pieces welded together with lead—and also to *insertis* and *iniunctis* (things joined and encased). These two series therefore reduce the differences to the indissolubility of things (or its absence), which results in the disappearance of the thing and thus of the *dominium* over the thing.

Oportet fiet (?) scilicet quia in specificatis ut in satis, in plantis, in ferruminatis, quia in hiis dominium discedit a quondam domino agi tantum actio in factum ad precium idest in pictura secundum quosdam [...] at in iniunctis, in inclusis, in aplumbatis, in insertis, in similibus agi tantum ad exhibendum ut separetur, ut eadem lege praeterquam in tingno ... nam tingnum et omnia ea quoque modo separata vendicantur in quibus dominium non abscessit.

[About the products of a specification, such as things sowed, planted, or united by *ferruminatio*, since the former owner loses all property rights, one must initiate an action *in factum ad precium* only, which, according to some, applies to paintings (...). However, when things are joined, incrusted, united by *adplumbatio*, encased, and similar situations, one must exclusively initiate an action *ad exhibendum* for separation, given that they are governed by the same law, except for construction timber . . . In fact, construction timber and all properties separated in any way can be claimed: in their case, there is no extinction of the property rights.][14]

Thus, *specificatio, ferruminatio, plantatio*, and *satio* constitute a single category governed by the idea that either the object disappears (the vessel incorporates its handle) or the things they affect cannot be separated without destruction. On the contrary, things that are *adplumbatae*, as well as *insertis* and *iniunctis*, can be separated while retaining a definite form, so that the things and the *dominium* both subsist.

The theme of *specificatio* will later be evoked by Bartolo, very probably quoting Rainiero da Forlì, one of his masters, who resorted to it, only to say the latter is wrong, because he understands the logic of the *media sententia* backward: that principle gives ownership of the thing to he who was the agent of its transformation when the object became no longer reducible to its primary substance, whereas Rainiero seems to affirm that reducibility brings ownership to the creator of the new *species*. The argument about the difference between painting and writing is that "scriptura non potest ita commode separari a charta sicuti pictura a tabula" (one can separate the painting from the tablet more easily than the writing from the *charta*). If we envisage the idea of inseparability as an avatar of *specificatio*, it is true that Rainiero's statement could be read thus: writing must appertain to the *charta*, because they cannot be separated, which means that the specified thing belongs to *dominus materiae* when it cannot recover its primary form. With a painting, on the contrary, which can be separated, the *tabula* must appertain to the painting, because it is reducible (in this case, we must understand that it is capable of being detached or separated). Read in this way, Rainiero's statement does interpret the *media sententia* backward.[15] We saw that Placentin also applied the *media sententia* to the *tabula picta* in a statement that, in truth, is infrequent.

The reasons for a supposed irreducibility, which are at the heart of the *media sententia*, are not stable. We see, for example, in the commentary to Johannes Faber's *Institutes*,[16] that the principle of irreducibility, which he otherwise rejects, is stated in terms of occupation of the surface, whereas the irreducibility discussed in D.41.1.7.7–8[17] is that of the return of a *species* to the state of *materia*, and that discussed by Rainiero da Forlì is grounded in the impossibility of a separation. For some, says Johannes Faber, painting covers the surface of the board in a way writing cannot, and that fully covered surface entails a mutation of the form, since "nihil apparet nisi pictura." He will reject this argument:

Quidam dicunt et attribuitur Jac. de Ra. quod in scriptura tota substantia non mutatur cum sit spatium inter literas lineas et dictiones sed in picturis ex toto mutatur ita quod nil apparet nisi pictura: et sic perinde est ac si non esset [. . .] et sic videtur forma mutata. Hec non videtur bona ratio: cum substantia tabule remanet et posset ad rudem materiam reduci coloribus abrasis. et nulla videtur transformatio per quam dominium deberet admitti [. . .] Praeterea possibile est totam tabulam non pingi vel dimitti spatium inter picturas.

[Some advance—this is an argument attributed to Jacques de Révigny[18]—that, in the case of writing, the substance does not change completely, since the letters, the lines, and the words have blank spaces between them, whereas in paintings the substance changes completely, because one can see only the painting, and thus it is as if it (the substance) did not exist, so a change in form seems to have taken place. However, this reasoning does not seem acceptable, because the substance of the tablet subsists and could be returned to the state of raw matter if one scraped off the colors. And no transformation seems capable of imposing the renouncement of one's property right. (. . .) Furthermore, the board may not be entirely painted or blank spaces may have remained between the colors.][19]

This idea of the fully covered surface was, in fact, used by Bartolo, but he interpreted it differently, linking it to the logic of the part and the whole, because Bartolo did not retain *specificatio* as the framework within which to inscribe writing and painting.[20] For him, *specificatio* governs neither the uniting of inks to *chartae* or parchments, nor colors to the *tabula*.

Thus, based on these understandings of *specificatio*—Placentin's, Jean Bassian's, and Rainiero's according to Bartolo, as well as Jacques de Révigny's according to Johannes Faber—the word does not name the same reality. For the first, the conditions for the creation of a new species are the dignity of the subject represented, the use of good colors carefully prepared, and the respect of pictorial skills—not the logic of the transformation of substances. One should also add the stage of completion of the work, which is one of the recurrent criteria in assessing the ripeness of the *specificatio* process, since mention of lime or ink may signal an incomplete or hastily crafted work. When those conditions are present, *specificatio*—thought of as a birth—takes place.

For Jean Bassian, *specificatio* is assimilated to the principle of cessation of a thing's existence and to the forms of theoretical inseparability, an idea that will reappear in Accursio's ordinary gloss. For Placentin, for Jacques de Révigny, according to Johannes Faber, and for Rainiero (at least as Bartolo reads him), reflection focuses on the relationship between the new *species* and its matter; and, as stated by the jurist Paul[21]—whose conclusions are reversed if one accepts the consequences of Rainiero's thinking, but which were correctly interpreted by Placentin—the object belongs to the owner of the substance if it can be reduced to it. If, on the contrary, there is excess, irreducibility of the thing to the substance, it must belong to him who performed the *specificatio*, thus granting him *dominium* over that thing which previously belonged to no one ("antea nullius fuerat"), according to Proculus's premises.

However, we must now return to Francesco Lucrezi's statement about D.50.16.13 and 14, and the syntagma "rem abesse videri." This will allow us to discuss the issues associated with the transformation of things by way of *operae*, the relationship between the form and the being of a thing, and that between name and form. We have highlighted the jurists' autonomy when they discuss the issue of *specificatio* as a process that gives rise to the *dominium* and that of the existence of a *species* endowed with a form that confers a name upon it. We must now highlight some points of contact between those two issues arising from the medieval texts.

Chapter 4

Form, Being, and Name

We must now return to D.50.16.14, a fragment by Jurist Paul, which states, as we have seen:

Labeo et Sabinus existimant si vestimentum scissum reddatur, vel res corrupta reddita sit: veluti sciphi collisi: aut tabula rasa pictura: videri rem abesse: quoniam earum rerum pretium non in substantia, sed in arte sit positum.

[Labeo and Sabinus think that if a garment is returned torn, or if a thing is returned corrupted, such as a broken vessel or a scratched painting, the thing is assumed to be absent, because the value of those things does not reside in their matter,[1] but in the art that produced them.]

A humanist addendum to the ordinary gloss states that the process of *specificatio* applies to the *tabula picta*, even if it restates that the *specificatio* dominates the matter in painting, but not in writing:

Id est plus constat specificatio quam valat materia: ut in tabula picta [. . .] unde Ovidius: Materiam superabat opus. Et contra quandoque minus: ut in litteris.

[That is to say, the specification has more power than the matter has value, as is the case with a painted tablet; (. . .) this is why, according to Ovid, work triumphs over matter. However, it sometimes is inferior to it, as is the case with writing.] (D.50.16.13 *Plus est*)

This excerpt is, to my knowledge, the only one evoking the existence of a *specificatio* rationale for writing in the context of the *tabula picta*—even though it denies it.

According to the Accursian gloss, the idea of a thing that is *mutata* applies as follows: "de materia in speciem: vel contra: vel de specie in speciem: vel prima facies deteriorata vel destructata est" (either a matter changed into *species*, or a *species* changed into *species*, either a first form deteriorated or destroyed), D.50.16.13; and also, at *Transfigurata*, "in aliam speciem." Odofredo reaffirms this interpretation. The extinction of the thing by *specificatio*, which allows one to qualify it as *transformata*, implies a cessation of existence (*esse desinit*) similar to that of dead things and things that stopped being *in rerum natura*.[2] This is true for things where the work is worth more than the matter: "plus est in manus pretio quam in re [...] nam opus aliquando superat materiam" (the price depends on the labor more than on the object [...] because labor sometimes prevails over matter).[3] In that case, the *specificatio* is the expression of the presence of art and technique, with one caveat: art must be strictly understood as a set of transformation skills, since Paul's text refers to garments, vessels, and paintings.

Strictly speaking, the problem of the thing that is *mutata* is that of form as the being of a thing, as dominating the material principle. In his *Summa* to the *Institutes*, Azo states:

Speciem factam intelligo etiam imperfectam ex quo rudis materiae nomen exuerit [...] et videtur quod in specificationis modo deficiat regula, meum est quod ex re mea superest, cuius vendicandi ius habeo [...] forte quia videtur res extincta, cum novam formam receperit: quia forma rei est esse rei.

[By *facta*, I mean a *species*, be it an unfinished one, stripped of the name for the unprocessed material (...) and a rule is obviously missing from the mode of specification: what remains of an object I owned belongs to me, and I have the right to claim it (...) it happens, in fact, that an object seems destroyed after being given a new form, because the form of an object constitutes the being of that object.] (*ad* 50)

The rationale points both to the naming and the form. The principle "forma rei est esse" responds to one of the fundamental principles of Aristotelian metaphysics. All material things are composed of two elements or principles: matter, which is the passive principle, the indeterminate element; and form, which is the active principle, the determinate element. Form can assume a permanent and fundamental modality, which places it inside a determinate *species*: this is the substantial form (the soul for humans or dogs); or it can be a variable and transitory modality, and the form is then accidental (for example, color, weight, position, etc.). One could cite numerous excerpts from Saint Thomas pointing that way:

Forma per seipsam facit rem esse in actu, cum per essentiam suam sit actus.

[The form suffices to render a thing actual, since its proper essence is to be actual.][4]

Cum omne esse sit a forma.

[Since all being draws its origin from a form.][5]

Forma dat esse et speciem.

[The form gives the being and the *species*.][6]

When he enunciates the principle "forma rei est esse rei," Azo refers to D.10.4.9.3, which states, "once the form is changed, the substance of the thing is almost destroyed" (nam mutata forma, prope interimit substantia rei). Yet the word "substance" raises a second issue. In Aristotelian vocabulary as well as in the vocabulary of scholastic theology, it first designates the quiddity of a thing, that by which it exists.[7] Nonetheless, Azo seems to cut through the philosophical discussion, as, in a gloss at *Substantiam* attributed to him, he states that the legal meaning of the word is different from its philosophical meaning and that one must construe it as the (legal) status of a thing, that is, what the thing is under the law, according to a rationale that considers the relationships between the form and the name of the thing, even if, in reality, its own definition of *substantia* is not very distant from the idea of quiddity.

There is a new *species*, Azo also states, as soon as the thing, even unfinished, can no longer be designated by the name of the unprocessed material; in that case, the word *factam* qualifies as the intermediary stage of transformation.[8] The thing always receives the name of the substance—wool, silver, gold—which no longer is raw wool or a mass of metal but is not yet fabric or vessel.

In effect, in excerpts from the *De verborum significatione* of the *Digest*, the issue of form is connected to naming. One should not forget that, in D.50.16.13 *Mulieris*, the excerpt by Ulpian on the thing that is *mutata* that ceases to be, opens with the following sentence: "under the name woman, one also includes the nubile virgin." The ordinary gloss explains that the word *mulier* can be used according to three modes: first, to name any female person, even a little girl; second, to name a woman who is *viripotens*, that is, a nubile woman, of at least twelve years of age; and third, only for the woman who is *corrupta*, no longer a virgin. The problem seems, therefore, to be one of naming, of the very precise relationship between the set of a thing's characteristics and its name. This is a fundamental problem, which must be taken into account in order to fully understand the reach of the *res abesse* syntagma.

In the *Tractatus de fluminibus seu Tyberiadis* attributed to Bartolo, written in 1335, we find a discussion of the concept of form and on the issue of naming. The form whose disappearance leads to the disappearance of the thing is solely the "propria forma rei," Bartolo explains. In doing so, he uses the Aristotelian categories of *forma substantialis* and *accidentalis*. The mutation of accidents does not eradicate the thing, the *species*, because it pertains to the form in its proper sense, that is, the substantial form. This substantial form is "per quod ipsa consistit: et vnde denominationem accipit, loquor de denominatione nominis appellatiui" (that which allows the stability of said *species*; it is from it that the *species* receives its denomination, I mean that denomination which is the appellative name). "According to the philosophers," that form is invisible in humans, the substantial form of which is the soul. However, one can hardly see the substantial form of wood, stone, or any other thing. Still, it is through accidental forms that we see, that we judge substantial form; thus, man has an organized body, and when he has that form we can say he has become man—the monster is not a man. The same goes for inanimate things; for example, we know earth because it has "the external accidents of earth"; if we turned the earth into "lapis coctus," having lost its own form, it would cease being earth, would become another *species*, and would lose its original name to assume another. It is the same for wine mixed with honey, which loses its accidents and becomes another *species* named *mulsum*. We can therefore conclude that inanimate things lose their substantial form when they lose their accidental form, from which they had derived their name, because the "nomina appellativa sunt immutabilia, stante scilicet identitate" (the appellative names are invariable, of course, because identity is stable). D.30.1.4 states that "rerum enim vocabula immutabilia sunt, hominum mutabilia" (terms that designate things are invariable; those that designate men are variable). In the case of things endowed with a vegetative soul, it is the latter's perdurability that defines existence; hence the tree, whose roots have dried, and that should be termed, strictly speaking, *lignum* if it is to be burned, or *materia* if it is to become construction lumber. Animals lose their substantial form when they lose their sensory mind, that is, when they become corpses. The man whose body is severed from his intellective soul when he passes away is also a corpse. The fifth category concerns "artificial" things that acquire their substantial form "ex quadam aptitudine, quam habent ad illum finem; ad quem per artifices factae sunt, vt domus" (from an aptitude they possess to fulfill the end for which craftsmen made them, as in the case of a house). Then, it is the adaptability to the final cause that defines existence, as is the case for vessels made for drinking or eating.[9]

One can also find that now common distinction between *materia, substantia*, and *forma* in Alciat:

Ex forma enim res ipsa nomen assumit: quapropter et ubi ea deest, rei quoque nomen deficit, nisi quid minimum de forma mutata proponatur [...] Materia est unde quid conficitur, ut in scypho metallum, in contractu consensus. Substantia est per quam materia in certam speciem deducitur, ut in vasis vel vestibus artificium, in emptionis contractu pretium. Forma est, quae certae illi speciei nomen dat.

[In effect, it is from its form that the thing itself derives its name: this is why, when that form no longer exist, the name of the thing also disappears, unless only a minute part of the modified form is visible to the eye . . . Matter is what allows an object to be made, such as metal for a vessel, a meeting of the minds for a contract. The substance is what allows matter to be shaped as a specific *species*, thus artifice for vessels or garments, price for a sale contract. Form is what gives its name to that specific form.][10]

It is unfortunately impossible to know if Bartolo believed that the inks and colors applied to a surface could be classified under one of those categories. However, it is probable that the answer would be negative, as we know that, for him, the rationale of *specificatio* did not apply *dominium* rights to painting or writing.

The naming theme also appears in a fragment from Ulpian we already mentioned, which concerns the legacy of books. As previously said, the issue involves the significance of words, of the "natura significationis verbis," according to Rogerius (twelfth century).[11] The word *libri* (D.32.52)[12] designates all the "volumina sive in charta, sive in membrana sint, sive in quavis alias materia," and also the *codices* made out of materials such as sheets of bark, linden tablets, and generally all membranes, animal or vegetable, and even wax and ivory tablets. Book legacy does not include the noninscribed *charta* or *membrana*, just as *chartae* legacy does not include books, and the word *membrana* does not designate any other writing support—this last statement about the difference between *chartae* and *membranae* is not accepted by the gloss, because, according to Rogerius, "membranas nostro vsu tantum chartas dicamus" (we are used to reserving the word *membranae* only for *chartae*) (D.32.52.4 *Non continebuntur*). However, the word *libri* does not include those whose writing has begun but is not finished, just as the word *vestis* does not include unfinished clothes. Although it is not necessary that it be adorned, glued, sewed, and corrected, it is however necessary that the object be entirely written to deserve being called a book. The gloss then indicates that there is a middle stage, a kind of suspension in a thing's process of transformation, that stops before the thing changes name and that causes a book that has been begun to evade the definitions of *chartae* or *libri*: "sic ergo libri coepti nec appellatione chartarum nec appellatione librorum continentur" (thus books that have been begun are not included under the name of *chartae*, nor under the name of books) (D.32.52.5 *Et non puto*). The same applies to the word *charta*, which does not include papyrus prepared for manufacture, as it only applies to "chartae . . . perfectae."[13]

Thus, issues around the law of *specificatio* and that of *appellatio* occasionally meet, even if they arise in different contexts. However, this is not systematic. Actually, if one accepts the consequences of D.50.16.13 and 14 for the *tabula picta*, as well as what is stated about the label "books" in D.32.52, one could believe painting and writing definitely find their place among things that acquire a new *species*. In fact, such is not the case, and it is important to note that the words *librum* and *imago* do not appear in the Justinian fragments about the *tabula picta*. When they do appear, they are associated with the issue of naming, that is to say, with what the words mean, and this naming issue is also that of the form as the being of the thing. This separation will deeply mark the gloss and commentary. Accordingly, naming is not subsumed by the rationale of appropriation, union, and separation of things. We must therefore return to these in order to identify the criteria mobilized by the major categories of *accessio* and *specificatio*.

Chapter 5
Ferruminatio, Adplumbatio

Ferruminatio unites iron to iron by means of iron, silver to silver with silver. The result is a continuity of substance, a full and definitive coherence. *Adplumbatio*, on the contrary, unites without continuity of substance.

[Cassius] dicit enim, si statuae suae ferruminatione iunctum bracchium sit, unitate maioris partis consumi: et quod semel alienum factum sit, etiamsi inde abruptum sit, redire ad priorem dominum non posse. Non idem in eo, quod applumbatum sit: quia ferruminatio per eandem materiam facit confusionem, plumbatura non idem efficit.

[(Cassius) says in fact that, if an arm is attached to its statue by *ferruminatio*, it is absorbed into the greater part because of its unity, and, once it belongs to another, that even if it (the arm) is torn apart, it cannot return to the previous owner. It is not so with respect to what was *applumbatum*: since *ferruminatio*, by means of matter itself, produces a fusion, whereas this does not happen by means of the *plumbatura*.] (D.6.1.23.5)

In the ordinary gloss relating to this excerpt, it says, at *Materia*:

Vt ferrum ferro, mediante ferro: argentum argento, mediante argento. et in similibus. Quodcumque autem istorum defuerit, erit applumbatum: aut hic euidenter dicit. ideo forte sic dicta, et quia per plumbum plerumque fit.

[Like (the union of) iron with iron by means of iron, of silver with silver by means of silver, and in similar cases. All that is not part of it will be "applumbatus," it is said clearly here. And this union is so named randomly or because most of the time it is performed using lead.]

In the Great Gloss, *ferruminatio* is assimilated to things that are sowed, planted, nourished by nature and to the *specificatis*:

Id est in hoc casu de ferruminatis [...]. Vel dic in omnibus his et similibus: vt satis, et naturali alimento alitis et specificatis secundum nos.

[That is to say in the case of elements united by *ferruminatio*. In our opinion, you should rather say: in all those cases and similar cases, for example in the case of things that are planted, of bodies that are nourished from food found in nature, and of things that result from a specification.] (D.6.1.23.5 *In omnibus*)

A coherence of parts is implied when one would make of them a thing contained "uno spiritu," Pomponius says (D.41.3.30)—"id est una elemen-tatione," the ordinary gloss proposes (D.6.23.5 *Vno spiritu*). The arguments drawn from the opposition between *ferruminatio* and *adplumbatio* to approach writing and painting are important in the work of gloss and commentary writers. In order to understand them better, we must focus briefly on two topics: the Roman tripartition of *corpora*, and the forms of union and mixture of substances. In Roman law, there exist a tripartition of *corpora*, a fundamental classification in which the jurists resort to Aristotelian and stoic concepts, which will, in turn, determine the definition of all that relates to the union of substances and *species*: *ferruminatio* and *adplumbatio*, *confusio*, *commixtio*, but also *specificatio*.

About usucaption (acquisition by prolonged possession), Pomponius enumerates three categories of *corpora* (D.41.3.30). The first *genus* is composed of those that "continetur uno spiritu," such as man, construction timber, and stone: "homo, tignum, lapis, et similia." In the gloss, *Similia* "et dicuntur species, vel indiuidua [. . .] in ista non cadit rerum mixtura" (it concerns *species*, and indivisible things [. . .] things that are mixed do not come under this category).

The second type concerns "quod ex contingentibus, hoc est pluribus inter se coharentibus constat" (what is constituted of elements that touch, that is several elements tied together), such as a building, a boat, a wardrobe. The terminology is nonetheless uncertain, as Paul (D.6.1.23.5) qualifies a simple thing "quod continetur uno spiritu" as *ex cohaerentibus*. The most common form of action they support is *tignum iunctum*, that is, the action for construction materials that retain their individuality, even if they cannot be reclaimed as long as the construction stands. It is also the case for parts of a statue united to the whole (or what amounts to the whole) by *adplumbatura*.

Finally, there is "quod ex distantibus constat: vt corpora plura [non] soluta, sed vni nomini subiecta: veluti populus, legio, grex" (what is made of discontinuous elements, like the numerous things that are [not] dissociated, but united under a single name, for example a people, a legion, a flock); according to Pietro Bonfante,[1] the "not" must be suppressed, because this is contrary to what Seneca says, who speaks of *corpora separata*, and it is consistent with the gloss: *Non soluta* "Immo soluta vere sunt, sed non soluta quo ad dispositionem patrisfami. et hoc dicitur vniuersitas" (on the contrary, they are indeed dissociated, but "not dissociated" because they form a whole from the standpoint of the family's father's management).

Quaedam continua corpora esse, ut hominem; quaedam esse composita, ut navem, domum, omnia denique, quorum diversae partes iunctura in unum coactae sunt; quaedam ex distantibus, quorum adhuc membra separata sunt, tamquam exercitus, populus, senatus. Illi enim, per quos ista corpora efficiuntur, iure aut officio coharerent, natura diducti et singuli sunt.

[There are homogeneous bodies, such as man; composite bodies, such as a ship, or a house, and finally and generally what owes its unity to the joining of separate parts; others are formed of discontinuous elements, and their parts remain separate: thus an army, a people, a senate. In fact, the parts that constitute these bodies, tightly linked by the law of their social function, exist by their nature separately and individually.][2]

The philosophical origin of the tripartition of the *corpora* can be found in the gloss, which mentions an excerpt from Seneca in connection with Pomponius's text. At *uno Spiritu*, the gloss states: "id est una elementatione, sive compagine elementorum non soluta: [. . .] Io. ut et ait Seneca: Omne quod undique suis partibus circumscribitur, vivere uno spiritu dicitur" (that is to say, formed of one element only, or of an assemblage of elements which are not dissociated [. . .] Io. declares, as Seneca says: *It is said that any body whose parts delineate all contours lives by virtue of a unique* spiritus).[3] Sextus provides the longest text on this issue.[4] The bodies, he writes, divide into three categories: those that are unified (*henoména*); those that are made of joined elements (*ek synaptoménon*); and those made of separate elements (*ek diestóton*). Bodies of the first type owe their unity to the strength of their *héxis*, as is the case for vegetables and animals. The second group of bodies is that of objects made out of diverse elements, such as chains, trunks, and ships. The third includes the ensembles formed by elements that are not joined together, such as armies, flocks, and choirs. In turn, this first tripartition is completed by a second division, which distributes the first type of bodies (unified bodies) into inert, vegetable, and animate.[5] However, this second tripartition seems indifferent to the legal texts, and Pomponius's enumeration includes all three categories: man, stone, construction lumber—provided the original state of the construction lumber is vegetable. The excerpt from Pomponius undoubtedly is related to the stoics, but the Aristotelian concept of "one" could equally bear on the understanding of this excerpt. Indeed, it is in Aristotle that one can find justification for the formula that designates *ex distantibus* bodies as being "vni nomini subiecta" (subjected to the same name).[6]

I neither intend nor feel competent to assess the role of philosophical traditions in classical Roman law, but I would like, nonetheless, to digress briefly on the conceptions of "one" proposed by Thomas Aquinas in his commentary to Aristotle's *Metaphysics*.[7] This text will allow us to apprehend, on a metaphysical plane, the legal classification of the *corpora*.

For Saint Thomas, there are five modes of the "one." The first one implies continuity (*natura continuitatis*). This continuity can be *secundum se* or *per aliud*. *Per aliud* applies, for example, to the bundle of wood or of pieces of wood:

Continua per aliud sunt, sicut onus lignorum continuum est ratione ligaminis vel vinculi: et hoc modo ligna adinvicem conviscata dicunt unum per viscum.

[There exist bodies that owe their continuity to a foreign bond; thus, a bundle of wood owes its continuity to a strap or a tie; similarly, one says that pieces of wood glued together are one due to the glue.]

What is "one" by nature is more one than what is rendered so artificially:

Magis unum sunt quae sunt continua per naturam, quam quae sunt continua per artem: quia in his quae sunt continua per naturam, illud unum, per quod fit continuatio, non est extraneum a natura rei quae per ipsum continuatur, sicut accidit in his quae sunt unum per artificium, in quibus vinculum, vel viscum, vel aliquid tale est omnino extraneum a natura colligatorum.

[Bodies that are continuous by nature are more united than bodies that are artificially continuous, because natural continuity of bodies is not owed to an element that is foreign to their nature, as is the case for bodies that are united artificially: a tie, glue, or any link of that sort is totally foreign to the nature of the bodies they hold together.]

Continuity *secundum se* excludes the notion of contact, which applies, rather, to continuity *per aliud*:

Illa sunt secundum se continua quae non dicuntur unum per contactum . . . alia unitatis continuorum, et alia tangentium.

[Bodies that are continuous *secundum se* are not those called "ones" as the result of a contact . . . The first unity is that of the continuous elements, the other is that born of elements that touch each other.]

This definition of unity as two modes of continuity, natural and artificial, is reminiscent of the two first categories of bodies, as they are envisaged by the law. Man, construction timber, and stone are continuous by nature; buildings, ships, wardrobes become bodies (*cohaerent*) artificially. Besides, the modes of material composition of things may vary. Among the "differentias accidentales rerum sensibilium" (the accidental variations of sensory bodies) are the modes of composition of the material parts. Some "componuntur per modum mixtionis, sicut mellicratum" (are composed by means of a mixing, such as mead), others "ligantur aliquo vinculo, sicut est ligatura capitis mulieris" (are tied by a bond, such as hair tied on a woman's head), and others yet "coniunguntur aliqua colla vel visco, sicut in libris" (are assembled by glue or pitch, as is the case for books), finally others "adunantur partes clavo, sicut fit una arca" (have their parts joined by a nail, like a wardrobe), or even mixing various modes.[8]

In the second mode of the "one," the substrate is not "specifically" different (which is to say due to the *species*). Some things can, indeed, be continuous while being diverse in their substrate due to the *species*.

Quaedam enim esse possunt continua quae tamen in subiecto sunt diversa secundum speciem; sicut si continuetur aurum argenti, vel aliqua huiusmodi. Et tunc talia duo erunt unum si attendatur sola quantitas, non autem si attendatur natura subiecti.

[Some bodies can, indeed, be continuous, even though their substrate is made of elements from diverse *species*, for example if gold is made continuous with silver, or in other such cases. And then both elements of that sort will make but one from the standpoint of quantity, but not from the standpoint of the nature of the substrate.]

This distinction allows us to understand both the second category of bodies and the specific issue of *ferruminatio* and *adplumbatio*.

The third mode is that of unity of *genus*, to the extent one can say man, horse, and dog are "one" according to their genre.

The fourth and fifth modes relate to unity of *ratio*, of *definitio*, that is to say, according to the quiddity.

Dicit quod unum etiam dicuntur, quaecumque ita se habent quod definitio unius, quae est ratio significans quid est esse, non dividitur a definitione alterius, quae significat etiam quid est esse eius.

[We also call "one," says he, bodies such as the definition of one, that is, the reason exhibiting its quiddity, is not divided by the definition of the other, which also exhibits its quiddity.]

Depending on the definition, the "one" can apply to diverse things, such as the ox and the horse, which are one by the definition of the animal, or to the "one" whose quiddity is absolutely indivisible. This indivisibility of the "one" according to the *ratio*, the *definition*, allows one to understand what Saint Thomas designates as derivative modes. Some pluralities are called "one" because they "faciunt unum; sicut plures homines dicuntur unum, ex hoc quod trahunt navem" (make one; one says, for example, that several men make one because they pull a barge). Others "ex eo quod unum patiuntur; sicut multi homines sunt unus populus, ex eo quod uno rege reguntur" (because they experience the same situation; thus a large number of men form a single people, because a single king rules over them). Others, because they hold something as "one," such as when multiple owners of a field are "one" in terms of the *dominium*. Others, finally, because they "are" one, just as all white men are because of their color. These derivative forms, which approach plurality as unity because they "faciunt unum," "unum patiuntur," "habent aliquid unum," or "sunt aliquid unum," send us back to indivisibility according to the *ratio*, the *definitio*, and allow us to understand the third type of bodies, bodies that are "ex distantibus," such as people, legions, or flocks. This digression into Aristotelian categories as interpreted by Thomas Aquinas shows that the tripartition of *corpora*, as conceived by medieval jurists and in particular by the commentary writers, could be enlightened by fragments from Seneca, and even more by Aristotle, whose authority was essential.

However, in reality, if the *corpora* are three in number, the operations of union, welding, or fusion produce four different forms of contact between things, which, incidentally, only concern the first two categories of objects. We will leave aside the third category, that of *corpora ex distantibus*, which the gloss writers call *universitas rerum* or *corporea*, or *universitas facti*—in contrast with *universitas iuris* or *incorporea*—of which the classical example is the flock, a thing always distinct and diverse from the sum of its components and constructed by subrogation. Construction by subrogation, in a fragment from Alfenus, at Book 6 of the *Digest*, actually designates all types of bodies, and not only the *corpora ex distantibus*.

Et legionem eandem haberi, ex qua multi decessissent, quorum in locum alii subiecti essent: et populum eundem ex illis nemo nunc viveret: itemque navem, si adeo saepe refecta esset, ut nulla tabula eadem permaneret quae non nova fuisset, nihilo minus eandem navem esse existimari. quod si quis putaret partibus commutatis aliam rem fieri, fore ut ex eius ratione non ipsi non idem essemus qui abhinc anno fuissemus, propterea quod, ut philosophi dicerent, ex quibus particulis minimis consisteremus, hae cottidie ex nostro corpore decederent aliaeque extrinsecus in earum locum accederent. quapropter cuius rei species eadem consisteret, rem quoque eandem esse existimari.

[A legion remains the same, even though many of its men might have died and others might have been brought in; a people that has no surviving member today remains the same; similarly, if a boat was rebuilt so often that there is not a single plank that is not new, we still regard it as the same boat. And let us imagine that, when its parts change, a body becomes another: under that reasoning, we would not ourselves be who we were a year before, because, according to the philosophers, we are made of minuscule particles, some of which leave our body every day, while others come from the outside to replace them. This is why, when the *species* of a body remains the same, we consider that the body also remains the same.] (D.5.1.76)

Universitas, that fundamental category in medieval political and institutional thinking, never applies to the *tabula picta*.[9]

Let us now see the different forms of union of substances and *species*. *Ferruminatio*, in the strict sense, must be distinguished from the category that merely applies to a theoretical inseparability that, according to the authors, allows for the substitution of objects such as painting, to the extent that it can be removed without damage and even without disappearance of its form. *Ferruminatio* as the union of two bodies made out of the same matter, by way of an identical substance, or as union of diverse bodies of a similar nature,[10] leads to a substantial coherence that links originally distinct objects to a single body endowed with internal force, *uno spiritu* content, or, according to the gloss, *una elementatione*. On the contrary, *adplumbatio*, by linking distinct parts, allows for the conservation of the resulting bodies in the second *genus rerum*: "Speciei coniunguntur nulla alia materia mediante puta ferrum ferro, argentum argento, aurum auro, alia materia non mediante coniungitur, uel conflatur" (One unites *species* without the means of another substance; for example iron and iron, silver and silver, gold and gold are united or melted together without the means of another substance).

Ferruminatio—the union of iron to iron—must be distinguished from *confusio* and from *commixtio*: *confusio* designates the mixing of *infectae* substances that make a single mass,[11] whether or not they constitute a new *species*; for example, there is *confusio* in the union of two pieces of melted gold, but no new *species* if the result is a formless mass, where only quantity has changed. *Commixtio* designates the union of bodies that retain their original *species* while forming a single and hardly separable body, as for mixed varieties of wheat.

The opposition *factum-infectum* is one of the criteria for the union of substances, since the *ferruminatio-adplumbatio* pair comes into play for things that are *factae*, while for things that are *infectae*, the *commixtio-confusio* pair operates in a mode of mixing substances and *species* that can occasionally lead to *specificatio*. Essentially, while *ferruminatio* and *adplumbatio* weld two things that retain a definite form, *confusio* and *commixtio* mix liquid or solid things of unstable or fluid form.

A fragment from Ulpian discusses these categories in detail. The series includes *commixtio* (for mixed wheat and mixed silver and lead), *confusio* (for mixed bronze and gold), *specificatio* (for *mulsum*), the act of *coalescere* (for the rooting tree), and progeny. Thus, the Roman world knows three modes of union for metals: they can fuse and create a new *species*, like silver and gold; they can mix while remaining distinct and capable of separation, like silver and lead; or they can fuse and become inseparable without producing a new *species*, like gold and bronze.

"Idem Pomponius scribit: Si frumentum duorum non voluntate eorum confusum sit, competit singulis in rem acti in id in quantum appareat in illo aceruo suum cuiusque esse. Quod si voluntate eorum commixta sunt, tunc communicata videbuntur: et erit communi diuidundo actio." "Idem scribit: si ex melle meo, et vino tuo, factum sit mulsum: quosdam existimasse id quoque communicari: sed puto verius vt et ipse significat eius potius esse, qui fecit: quoniam suam speciem pristinam non continet." "Sed si plumbum cum argento mixtum sit: quia deduci possit, nec communicabitur, nec communi diuidendo agetur, quia separari potest. [. . .] Sed si deduci, inquit, non possit: vt puta si aes, et aurum mixtum fuerit: pro parte esse vindicandum Nequaquam erit dicendum quod in mulso dictum est: quia vtraque materia, et si confusa, manet tamen." "Idem scribit, si equam meam equus tuus praegnantem fecerit, non esse tuum sed meum, quod natus est." "De arbore, quae in alienum agrum translata coaluit, et radices immisit: Varus et Nerua vtilem in rem actionem dabant, nam si nondum coaluit, mea esse non desinet."

["Similarly, Pomponius writes: If the wheat from two landowners is mixed without their agreement, each has rights over the result of the mixing, to the extent that it is clear that his own property is part of the mix. But if their goods are mixed with their agreement, then they will obviously be shared, and we will file an action for the sharing of the common good." "Similarly, he writes: if with my honey and your wine honey wine is made, some consider that this mix is common, but I think it fairer, as he states himself, that it belong to him who made it, since it does not retain its original *species*." "But if one alloys lead to silver, since the lead can be extracted, there will be neither commonality, nor action for the sharing of the common good, because separation is possible. (. . .) But he adds that if it is impossible to achieve retraction, for example if one alloys bronze and gold, it should not be said that such alloy will be claimed on a pro-rata basis, as was said about honey wine because the two substances subsist separately, despite the mixing." "Similarly, it is written that if your horse covers my mare, it is I and not you who will own the foal." "In the case of a tree that, after being carried to the field of another, roots and grows there, Varus and Nerva argued the utility of an action in restitution. In fact, if the tree has not yet rooted, it still belongs to me."] (D.6.1.5)

About D.6.1.5.2 *Vtraque*, the gloss will explain what distinguishes *commixio* from *confusio*. First, one says that *species* "misceri," while *materiae* "confundi"; then, that *species mixtae* retain a same substance and *species*, while *species confusae* "transferunt in aliam materiam"; finally, that the *confusa* belong in common to two owners, even without their will, but the *mixta* require their agreement. Yet, the excerpt also mentions that one frequently (and improperly) speaks of *confusio* for mixed wheat.

The tripartition of mixes originally proposed by Chrysippus (280 B.C.–ca. 200 B.C.) helps us better understand what included the categories of *ferruminatio, adplumbatio, confusio, commixtio,* and, to a certain extent, *specificatio.* I do not intend to make this text the origin of legal categories. It is mentioned herein only to clarify the processes that designate those categories. According to Alexander of Aphrodisias in his *De mixtione*,[12] Chrisyppus holds that some bodies are united "by juxtaposition" in the case where each substance it contains preserves its surface and quality in that juxtaposition, as is the case with mixed wheat. Others produce a total fusion of substances; their qualities cancel each other out and the result is another body, as is the case with medicine. Finally, others result in a mix in which the substances and their qualities are mutually coextensive in their totality and preserve their original substance and their qualities in that union. Therefore, there is either juxtaposition, or fusion and production of a new body, or mixing of substances that retain their identity. However, if Chrisyppus holds that all three can be unified by a same *pneuma*, legal texts hold that only certain bodies are contained *uno spiritu*, and the example of man corresponds to what Seneca designates as the continuous bodies.[13] The first type of mixing corresponds to *commixtio* and, on the surface of welded things, to *adplumbatio*; the second corresponds to *specificatio* if the original substances were different, and to *ferruminatio* on the surface of welded things; the third could allow us to understand *confusio*.[14]

The arguments drawn from the opposition between *ferruminatio* and *adplumbatio* to discuss writing and painting appear in Placentin's *Summa*, where the *tabula picta* is compared to *ferruminatio* and also to what grows roots in the ground. The language of *ferruminatio* is the same as that used for plants and seeds, and it produces the same effect as what becomes one with the soil—a tree growing roots into a soil is as if *ferruminata*, definitely united to it, even if, in that case, there is no disappearance of an object. *Adplumbatio*, on the contrary, is the union produced by another substance, and that solution of continuity makes it possible to reclaim the part that was joined at any time.

In this rationale of union by what is identical or by what is different, writing and painting constitute complex forms because, even though one cannot say there truly is *ferruminatio* in the absence of a continuity of substance, they share certain consequences related to the process: like things that are *ferruminatae*, once the paint or the ink has been erased, the support does not revert to its original owner, but, rather, remains part of the patrimony of the painter or the writer. One could perhaps say then that painted or inscribed objects share with *ferruminatio* the creation of coherence, of a body contained *una elementatione*; however, that coherence is achieved without identity of substances. Thus, *ferruminatio* is assimilated to what *coalescit*, what becomes one body; it is a form of insolubility, and it is as such that it can govern the relationship between paint, ink, and their respective supports. However, this insolubility is neither a true continuity of substances, nor a true "rooting" of the colored substances in the "soil" of their surface.

For Placentin, *ferruminatio*, to which one partially assimilates painted and written objects, in no way implies a new *species* as such or systematically. We have already noticed the fundamental originality of this author, continued and developed by Odofredo. In the case of painting, the creation of a new *species* depends on the quality of the work and the dignity of the painted forms, and in the case of writing, on the beauty of the lines drawn by the scribe's hand. In his reading of the *Institutes*, a few years after Placentin's *Summa*, Jean Bassian tightens the link between painting and *ferruminatio*. In fact, he revisits the issue raised by *ferruminatio* as one of the five elements that pertain to the specificity of the *tabula picta*: once the *tabula* is "abrasa," it does not revert to its original owner. Placentin finds this feature original, because painting was assimilated to things *ferruminatae* only with respect to the consequences of the process, but not as to their respective nature, painting being *ferruminata* only in its appearance. For Bassian, the rule by which the *tabula*, even when *abrasa*, could not revert to its owner prior to the painting was in no way original. On the contrary, this rule could be explained by the principle of extinction of the *dominium* relative to the added element, which took place as to things *ferruminatae*, but also as to sowing, planting, and specification—in opposition to things united by *adplumbatio*, such as construction timber, sleeves added to a garment, or things "joined . . . encased . . . inlaid." Paola

Maffei has edited three different manuscripts, one of which shows a corruption of the tradition, which had already been highlighted by Ennio Cortese.[15] This first manuscript contains a long gloss that Paola Maffei attributes to Bassian. It is this last text I am referring to; while enumerating the rules of procedure particular to painting, he states:

> Licet pictura non possit esse sine tabula non tamen cedit tabule, sed tabula picture ... dominus pla. [Placentin] dixit aliud esse speciale, quia tabula abrasa non ideo eam vendicabit directo, ego speciale non puto, sicut in aliis in quibus dominium discessit, ut in ferruminatis ut supra dictum est.

> [Even though a painting cannot exist without the tablet, it does not appertain to the tablet; it is, on the contrary, the tablet that appertains to the painting ... Master Placentin says there is another particularity: if the board is scraped, (its former owner) will not submit a *reivindicatio directa*; but to my mind, this is no particularity: the same is true in other cases of extinction of property rights, such as cases of union by *ferruminatio* mentioned above.][16]

This assimilation between *ferruminatio* and *tabula picta* becomes common. Nonetheless, in the fourteenth century, Alberico de Rosate (ca. 1290–1360) classifies painting and writing in the category of things *adplumbatae* ("diversa corpora eiusdem speciei, et naturae iunguntur mediante alia materia, quae non est eiusdem speciei"),[17] which, one could logically add, constitute a composite body, and not a simple body, defined *una elementatione*. Alberico de Rosate, although a prolific author, never taught. Born in Bergamo into a family of judges and notaries, he became famous as a *magnus practicus*; however, in the professorial style, he wrote commentaries to the *Digest*—very relevant to our theme—and to the *Codex*, as well as a *Dictionarium iuris*.[18] His long commentary to *Item quacumque* is of particular interest for several reasons.[19] First, Alberico is, to my knowledge, the only one who speaks of painting and writing in connection with *adplumbatio*, while all his predecessors approached painting and writing by analogy with *ferruminatio*. Second, he designates ink and paint as things that are *infectae* and their respective supports, *tabula* and *charta*, as things that are *factae*.[20] Finally, he refers to what the "artifices" say on this subject, and he adds a third mode of junction—which is mentioned in a gloss (D.32.50.9 *Et vinculis*) but without approaching it as a mode of union of bodies with a specific legal status—that of nailed things, such as for example the foot of a vase attached to it by small nails made of the same matter as the vase. This process is described in Theophilus's treatise, on the subject of the making and decorating of the saddle and bridle of a horse, the sheath of a knife, or leather bookbinding.[21] For Alberico, it is a union made by means of identical matter, but the added thing does not become extinct due to the uniting technique, which permits severance.

Let us return to *adplumbatio*. It concerns, says Alberico, the union of silver to silver or gold to gold using lead, of fabric to fabric using thread; the same applies to the *charta* and the writing, united by ink, and for *tabula* and painting, united by colors ("et pariter in charta, et scriptura, quae coniunguntur mediante incausto, et tabula, et pictura mediantibus coloribus"). This rather surprising text does not assume that *charta* and *tabula* are supports prepared using substances such as, for example, linseed oil, wax, or *album plumbum*, which, when mixed with wax, helped smooth the surface of the wood. This process is described in Book 3 of the *De Coloribus et Artibus Romanorum* by Eraclius.

Quomodo aptetur lignum antequam pingatur. Quicumque aliquod lignum ornare diversis coloribus satagis, audi quae dico. In primis ipsum lignum multum rade equalem, et planissimum radendo, et ad ultimum fricando cum illa herba quae dicitur asperella. Quod si ligni materies talis fuerit, ut non possis equare ejus asperitates, vel non velis, propter aliquas occasiones, nec tamen cum corio illud velis cooperire, vel panno; album plumbum teres super petram siccum sed non tantum quantum si inde pingere velis. Deinde ceram in vase supra ignem liquefacies, tegulamque tritam subtiliter albumque plumbum, quod ante trivisti, simul commisces, saepius movendo cum parvo ligno, et sic sine refrigerari. Postea aliquod ferrum fac calidum, et, cum ipso, ceram funde in ipsas cavernulas donec equales sint, et sic cum cultello desuper abrade ea quae sunt scabrosa. Si autem album plumbum miscere cum cera dubitas, scito quod tantum plus miscueris, tanto durius erit. Et, sicut dixit, jam equali facto, habundancius plumbum, valde subtilissime tritum cum oleo lini, desuper, per totum ubicunque pingere vis, tenuissime extendendo cum pincello asinino, sic aptato; deinde ad solem exsiccari bene permitte. At post, cum siccatus fuerit color, interdum superpone, sicut prius fecisti, de eodem, et spissiorem pones; sed non ita spissiorem, ut habundancius colorem superponas, sed ut oleum minus habeat. Nam et in hoc multum cavendum est ut nunquam crassiorem colorem superponas; quod si feceris et abunde posueris, cum exsiccari coeperit, rugae desuper erunt. Nunc autem ut ea quae supersunt simul omnia dicam, superius quaeso me redire permitte, ubi de ligni nuditate locutus sum, si illud corio vel panno operire volueris. Quod si lignum, quod pingere volueris, non fuerit equale, corio equino vel perchameno operi illud.

[How to prepare the wood prior to painting it. You who are trying to embellish wood with various colors, listen to my words! Start by planing said wood to make it regular and perfectly plane; finally polish it with the weed named *asperella*. If the substance of the wood prevents you from leveling its asperity, or you do not wish it because it is advantageous, and still you do not want to cover it with leather or cloth, rub a dry stone to extract white lead powder, but not as much as you would for painting. Then, you will melt the wax by placing a vessel over fire, you will mix into it a tile ground to a very fine powder as well as the previously prepared white lead powder; stir quite often with a small stick, and allow to cool off. After that, heat up iron and use it to pour the wax in the small cavities until they are level, and as follows, with a small knife, scrape the surface to remove the bumps. If you hesitate as to the mix of white lead and wax, remember that the more lead you add, the harder the mix. And, as I said, when the wood is already smooth, prepare it as follows: take a large enough amount of extremely fine lead powder mixed with linseed oil and, with a donkey-bristle brush, spread it in a very thin layer over the entire area to be painted; then let it dry in the sun. Afterwards, when the color is dry, as you did previously, lay a new, thicker layer; that does not mean you will apply a larger quantity of color, but that it will contain less oil. In fact, you must be very careful never to apply too thick a layer of color: if you do so and apply too abundant a layer, a roughness will appear on the surface from the start of the drying process. And now, to gather all I still have to say, allow me, I beg you, to repeat what I said earlier about the raw wood, in case you would like to cover it with leather or fabric. If the wood you would like to paint is not smooth, cover it with horse leather or parchment.][22]

Painting is never applied on a rough board; on the contrary, it must be prepared and, in some cases, covered with fabric—or less often leather—to even the surface and provide a more flexible support. Here, Alberico does not seem to refer to a process that would suggest a parallel between those preparatory materials covering the surface, like lead or thread, as a sort of welding, junction, intermediary layer between the *tabula* and the colors. On the contrary, he affirms the separation between the *scriptura*, the *pictura*, and the substance—ink or color—by means of which writing or painting comes to exist. However, Alberico does not deduce from this any immateriality or abstraction of the writing and the painting. Following his rationale, we are indeed talking about two bodies united by means of another substance. This deeply original construction thus seems to imply that each particular writing or painting envisaged as *species*, as individuated, is united to its support by means of ink and colors, yet without any fusion, and without legal extinction of one of the bodies. Like many others, after having reviewed the various rationales governing the relationship between substance and form, Alberico reverts to a classical decision and accepts value as the critical element, capable of breaking away from the reasons that logically order things among themselves.

However, Alberico's text highlights the random quality of this rationale: nothing compels us to include painting and writing in the group of things united by a principle of sameness, nor to accept that union by a different substance produces a temporary coherence. Also, nothing compels us to approach a concrete written text or a painting in its singularity, as a body united for the sole reason that any separation would necessarily destroy it. For him, they seem to be objects made of successive layers: the support, the ink or colors, the writing or painting in its particular form, two things joined by means of a third, substantially different thing.

Chapter 6
Factae *and* Infectae

None of the three fragments from the Justinian corpus applied the categories of things that are *factae* and *infectae* to painting and writing, but Odofredo and Alberico do, to designate the relationship between colors, ink, the *tabula* and the *charta*. The opposition also is at the center of the gloss at D.6.1.23. That excerpt deals with the adjunction of a part to whatever can be designated as a whole: an arm added to a statue, a handle added to a vessel, a leg added to a table, and so on. This rule of absorption of the part by the whole only applies, the gloss states, when silver that is *factum* is added to silver that is also *factum*, for if one adds *infectum* to *infectum*, neither appertains to the other, and the resulting mass becomes common property if it cannot be separated. Coming back to our starting point, if one deals with the adjunction of *factum facto*, but none can appertain to the other as a part—that is, as a specific part with a name, handle, foot, arm, but whose absence would not prevent the thing from being a "species per se": "erat ergo statua species per se etiam sine adiuncto" (the statue was therefore a *species* on its own, even without the addition, D.6.1.23.2 *Statuae*)—then the larger part is increased by the smaller. If the two parts are equivalent, the value will define the rule of *accessio*: the higher-valued part attracts the lower-valued one. Finally, when a substance that is *facta* is adjoined to a substance that is *infecta*, the first one dominates, provided the mode of junction results in inseparability, meaning they are joined by *ferruminatio*.[1]

However, what is the significance of the *factum* and *infectum* categories? Can one regard all man-made things as *facta* and all raw substances as *infecta*? We will see that, if the latter is true, it does not follow that the former is. Labor, human hands, and the operations of transformation and manufacture do not always imply a qualification of *factum*. For example, a legacy that includes silver that is *factum* does not include coins, which means that minting is an operation excluded from the concept of *factum*. Nor does *factum* apply to silver or gold categorized as *supellex*. "Supellex est domesticum patris familiae instrumentum, quod neque argento aurove facto vel vesti adnumeretur" (the *supellex* is the furniture of the house and belongs to the head of family; one would not adjoin it to silver or gold that is *facto*, nor to garments, D.33.10.1). That is to say all that can be considered as part of the daily things of a *pater*, but is not part of another specific category, such as food supply, silverware, wardrobe, jewelry, or the equipment of a plot or house. This means that gold or silver pieces that have been wrought and encased or inlaid on furniture are outside of that category of *factum*: "Argentum factum recte quis ita definierit, quod neque in massa, neque in lamina, neque in signato, neque in supellectili, neque in mundo, neque in ornamentis sit" (It would be right to define silver that is *factum* as follows: it is neither a mass, an ingot, minted coins, *supellex*, jewelry, or ornaments, D.34.2.27.6). In the *Pauli Sententiae* 3.6.88, silver that is *factum* is part of the *genus ornamentorum*.

The *factum* category seems, therefore, to point toward certain operations that produce:

—utensils made of silver or gold;
—objects that can be used to contain various solid or liquid substances, as well as other supporting objects, such as saucers or trays (D.34.2.18.10); the idea of making the convenient use of a thing part of its definition is in an excerpt from Ulpian (D.34.2.27.3): "Cui aurum vel argentum factum legatur si fractum vel collisum sit, non continetur. Servius enim ita existimat aurum vel argentum factum id videri: quo commode uti possumus: argentum autem fractum vel collisum non incidere in eam definitionem, sed infecto contineri" (a legacy of gold or silver that is *factum* does not include the occasional broken or dented objects. Servius opines, in effect, that one considers as being *factum* only gold and silver we can conveniently use; however, according to him, broken or dented silver does not fit this definition and belongs to silver that is *infectum*);[2]
—objects that can be included into the *vasa* category, but which exclude, for example, all kitchen utensils (D.34.2.18.12): "Argento facto legato, Quintus Mucius ait, vasa argentea contineri: veluti parapsides, cetabula, trullas, pelves, et his similia, non tamen quae supellectilis sunt" (according to Quintus Mucius, a legacy of silver that is *factum* includes silver vessels, such as trays, saucers, pitchers, caldrons, and similar objects, but not those that are part of the *supellex*, D.34.2.18.9).

This category, however, does not concern only silver and gold. It is applied to wool for garments, and the commentary writers will extend it to other objects, other materials, such as construction timber, the *tabula*, or sculpted marble. Yet, a thing need not be finished to be considered *facta*.

Infecti autem argenti appellatio rudem materiam continet, id est non factam. Quid ergo si coeptum sit argentum fabricari, nondum perfectum? Vtrum facti, an infecti appellatione contineatur, dubitari potest. Sed puto magis facti.

[Under the phrase "silver that is *infectum*," one includes raw material, that is to say, not processed. What about silver upon which work would have been started but not yet finished? One can hesitate to include it under the term *factum* or *infectum*, but I rather think it is silver that is *factum*.] (D.34.2.19.11)

However, if manufacture in process generates the label of *factum*, subsequent destruction, even partial, leads to destruction of the object as such.

From these definitions, it ensues that the *factum* category not only applies to all labor on a mass of matter or all forms of manufacture. An excerpt from Paul explains the preferential use of the *factum-infectum* categories with metal. Where metal is concerned, the power of the material prevails over that of the form. A metallic object can always be melted and return to the raw material, and, because of that, it never loses its name.

Illud fortasse quaesiturus est aliquis, cur argenti appellatione etiam factum argentum comprehendetur: cum, si marmor legatum esset, nihil praeter eundem[3] materiam demonstratum videri posset. Cuius haec ratio traditur: quippe ea quae talis naturae sint ut saepius in sua possint redigi initia, ea materiae potentia victa numquam vires eius effugiant.

[Perhaps one will ask why the name "silver" also includes silver that is *factum*, since when marble is bequeathed, one could think we are dealing only with the same substance. Here is the reason tradition gives: the nature of those objects quite often allows them to recover their original state, and, if the power of their material has been mastered, they rarely escape its properties.] (D.32.78.4)

Thus the words *factum-infectum* strictly apply to materials, the *specificatio* of which does not produce extinction. Wool, cypress wood, marble, says Accursio, are prevailed upon by the specified objects made from those materials and lose their name. *Factum* thus modifies a name that does not disappear.

Omnia enim metalla superant sua specificata, potentia: et quod nullo modo extinguuntur specificatione lana autem cypressus siue marmor vincuntur a suis spectatrices: cum ad sua ultra non redeant initia: et plerumque, ut lana et cypressus, et similia: ut farina nomen etiam perdunt. vel amitunt, metalla autem [. . .] ne nomen suum perdunt, nam si anulus est, non minus aureus vocatur: sed vestis nunquam lana: sicut nauis cypressi non cypressus dicitur.

[In fact, all metals prevail over the *species* they allow to be made because of their power and because the specification can never cause their extinction. By contrast, wool, cypress wood, or marble are prevailed upon by the *species* they generate, because they do not subsequently return to their original state; and most of the time, as is the case for wool, cypress wood, and similar bodies, such as flour, they also lose their name or shed it, whereas metals (. . .) do not lose their name. Indeed, if one speaks of a ring, one also speaks of "gold"; but if one speaks of a garment, one never speaks of "wool," just like a boat made of cypress wood is never named "cypress."] (D.32.78.4 *Victa*)

Or, as Bartolo states, "Appellatione materiae non continetur materiatum quod ad sui materiam reuerti non potest" (one does not apply the name of the material to an object that cannot revert to that [raw] material).[4] In reality, the word *facta* properly applies to wool when it is "carpinata, et pectinata, et batuta, et in manellis parata ad ponendum in tela" (spun, combed, dyed and spooled to be used on the loom, D.32.70.1 *Facta*).

This discussion about the potential of matter in the naming of things can be clarified by Aristotelian concepts. On several occasions,[5] Aristotle affirms that the substance-to-be, the one that holds a potential, gives its name to things. The name of the made thing will derive from the substance but will not be the substance itself. "It seems that what we are describing is not a particular thing, but a definite material; e.g., a box is not wood, but wooden material, and wood is not earth but earthen material; and earth also is an illustration of our point if it is similarly not some other thing, but a definite material—it is always the latter term in this series which is, in the fullest sense, potentially something else." "*Materia*, Thomas Aquinas writes in his commentary to the *Metaphysics, non praedicatur in abstracto de eo quod est ex materia, sed denominative*" (one does not give the name of the substance, *in abstracto*, to an object made from it, but rather a derivative name).[6] This interpretation, however, only partially reflects the statements of the law. The relationship between the potential of matter and naming is clarified, but not the idea that only certain materials cannot be prevailed upon by their specified forms.

We have seen that the Roman texts do not mention materials that are *factae* and *infectae* in terms of the issue of *tabula picta*. However, Odofredo does, and so does Alberico, as they give those categories a meaning different from that found in the Justinian excerpts. In his commentary to *Item quaecumque*

(D.6.1.23.5), Odofredo analyzes the relationship between materials that are *factae* and *infectae*. In that context, writing is used as an example of the relationship between my substance that is *infecta* joined to your substance that is *facta* "verbigratia: scribo in carta tua nunc iungo meam infectam tuae factae" (for example: I write on your *charta*: I am uniting my substance that is *infecta* to your substance that is *facta*).[7] In reality, Odofredo opts for the principle *charta cedit scripturae* in his praise of the art of writing, which he ranks well above painting; however, the reason for this cannot be based on the *factae* and *infectae* categories, since by this token the ink used to write, being *infecta*, should appertain to the support. Here, the opposition lies in the fluidity of materials. What distinguishes ink and paint from their supports is not the indomitable power of a substance always capable of prevailing over a transitory form, but their fluid and unstable nature.

Alberico expounds at length on this opposition and explains the difference between things that are *factae* and *infectae* as follows:

Et dicitur materia facta, quae habet formam siue sit perfecta, siue inchoacta tantum, et non perfecta, ut pote statua, scyphus, pes et manus. Materia autem infecta dicitur, quae non habet formam, sed est in rudi materia, sicut massa ferri, vel argenti, vel quae iam fuit facta sed modo est destructa, et reducta ad rudem materiam, sicut cum aliquod uas argenti, vel auri conflatur, et reducitur ad massam, ut hic probatur. Infra de auro et argento lega. l. et si non sunt. § argento facto et § infecti. [D.34.2.19.6 and 11] and l. quintus. § cui aurum et § si factum et § argentum factum. [D.34.2.27.3, 4 and 6].

[One calls *materia facta* that which has a form, be it perfected or only in process and unfinished, for example a statue, a vessel, a foot and a hand; one calls *materia infecta* that which has no form, but which is raw material, thus a mass of iron or silver, or that which has been *facta*, but is now destroyed and reduced to raw material, as when a silver or gold vase is melted and reduced to its mass.][8]

He mentions paint as an example of a substance that is *infecta* applied upon a surface regarded as *facta*. Inside this classification of the relations between *factae* and *infectae*, writing and painting appear, as with Odofredo, in the fourth case: when I add my substance that is *infecta* to your substance that is *facta*. For example, if I paint on your *tabula* "quae est materia facta" with my paint, categorized as *infecta*, or if I write on your *charta* with my ink, understood as *infecta*, assuming all was done in good faith, the price of materials will determine the ownership of the object.[9] This opposition does not seem to add much to the better-accepted others, such as that of value, of part and whole, of *ferruminatio* and *adplumbatio*. The criterion of materials that are *factae* and *infectae* always seems to yield to value, and its procedural consequences are made relative by the *ferruminatio-adplumbatio* opposition. However, this opposition nevertheless adds a particular way of approaching the materials for writing and painting, to the extent that colors and inks are considered as materials that are *infectae*, even though one cannot ignore that they result from a manufacturing process.

Thus, we have seen that the difference between *facta* and *infecta* does not refer only to the existence of a manufacturing process, to art as opposed to nature. The words seem to apply to the existence of a fixed form, perfect or incomplete; however, the fluid nature of a substance seems to make it *infecta*. Thus materials that are *facti* are, on the one hand, those which can retain a fixed form because of their solid nature, which ink or colors cannot achieve; on the other hand, these words—which are mostly used for materials, the nature of which may prevail over their specified forms—can designate various stages in the transformation process, for if combed and spun wool is regarded as "lana facta," once woven, it stops being wool to become fabric.[10]

The opposition *factum-infectum* incorporates painting and writing into a discussion about the fluidity of substances as a mode of formlessness, of the form that is about to be born and the material, even if, in the end, value will resolve and replace, once more, the dichotomous categories.

Chapter 7
Praevalentia

In an article on *specificatio,* Contardo Ferrini states that the Romans conceived of two original forms of acquisition of *dominium,* one being that of occupation, and the other they called "attraction of the *dominium.*" The Romans may have expressed that power of attraction of the *dominium* in sentences such as "what is built on a land appertains to the land" or "appertain to the *tabula* because of accession." Jurist Paul (D.6.1.23.3) probably best stated that "law of attraction" by stating that there is *accessio* when my thing attracts and makes mine the thing of another "per praevalentiam."[1] This law of attraction operates when a thing enters the *dominium* of another when that second thing incorporates the first, absorbs it, gets nourished by it, or even cancels the primal specificity of the added thing. In fact, this law governs what is regarded as a class of acquisition of *dominium,* which includes fruits and progeny (vegetables or animals appertaining to the owner of the plant or womb that produced them); and added things. *Praevalentia* thus implies the principle of appurtenance of a thing to that other thing without which the first could not exist: "necesse est ei rei cedi id, quod sine illa esse non potest." However for the gloss, the *praevalentia* does not require application of the principle *superficies solo cedit.*

Indeed, if one reads Paul in perspective; if one construes the sentence in the context of the preceding and following sentences, to which it is related by its own incipit, "sed et id," and by that of D.6.1.23.4: "In omnibus igitur istis"; if, finally, one adds the gloss and commentary excerpts by Bartolo, one can observe the emergence of the *praevalentia* rationale, linked to that of the part and the whole, with a touch of *pretium.* That is, the ensemble formed by the three following fragments:

Si quis rei suae alienam rem ita adiecerit, ut pars eius fieret; veluti si quis statuae suae brachium, aut pedem alienum adiecerit, aut scypho ansam, vel fundum, vel candelabro sigilum, aut mensae pedem: dominum eius totius rei effici: vereque statuam suam dicturum, et scyphum, plerique recte dicunt.

[If someone added a thing of another to his own, so that it becomes part of it, if for example he added an arm or a foot to a statue belonging to someone else, or a handle or a bottom to his vessel, or a figurine to his candlestick, or a leg to his table, he becomes the owner of the whole thing, and many affirm with reason that he will rightly claim that the statue or vessel belongs to him.] (D.6.1.23.2)

Sed et id, quod in charta mea scribitur, aut in tabula pingitur, statim meum fit: licet de pictura quidam contra senserint propter pretium picturae: sed necesse est ei rei cedi id, quod sine illa esse non potest.

[However what is written on my paper or painted on my board becomes mine immediately, although some believe otherwise as to painting, because of its price, but it is necessary that the thing appertain to that without which it cannot subsist.] (D.6.1.23.3)

In omnibus igitur istis, casibus in quibus mea res per preualentiam alienam rem trahit meamque efficit. Si eam rem vendicem, per exceptionem doli mali cogar pretium eius, quod accesserit, dare.

[Thus, in all cases where my thing attracts to it another's, it makes that thing mine (so long as it prevails); if I want to claim that thing under the bad faith exception, I will have to pay the price of that which has been added.] (D.6.1.23.4)

For the gloss, there exist two different postures at the outset. About *In omnibus*, Accursio reports two opinions: that of Io. (probably Jean Bassian), who states that the plural therein must be interpreted as a singular and that the idea expressed in the preceding excerpt, by which it is necessary that the thing appertain to that without which it cannot subsist, applies only to writing; and that of Azo, who believes, on the contrary, that the principle applies to the *statua* as well as to the *charta*.

Si talibus: vel plurale pro singulari casu: vt sic ad picturam non referatur, secundum Io. Vel dic vt statua, et charta, secundum Azo.

[About *talibus*: either the plural is used in place of the desinence of the singular, so that painting is not included, as is Johannes's opinion; or else you must say: "for example a statue and a *charta*, as is Azo's opinion."] (D.6.1.23.4 *In omnibus*)

If one adds the words that gloss the syntagma *Per praeualentiam* (D.6.1.23.4) to these excerpts, "partis, vel etiam pretij," three ways of interpreting this principle of attraction or absorption of a thing by another can be derived. Either it emerges from the idea of land, of a support that absorbs what has no autonomy, and it applies only to writing—which means, strangely, that painting could "float" without a surface to inscribe it on. Or it responds to the rationale of the part and the whole, also recognizing that only painting could avoid being part of a whole that supports it. Or it is the value that prevails, by annulling both the land criterion and that of the whole. The *praevalentia*, as understood by the gloss, retains both the rationale of the part and the whole, and that of the value; the first governs writing and statues, and the second, painting. Therefore, we must now focus on the evolution of those two criteria: the value rationale and the relationship between the whole and the part.

Chapter 8
Pretium *and* Pretiositas

For the gloss writers, orthodoxy with respect to the Justinian corpus on *tabula picta* may take three forms. Two of them concern hypotheses of logic and the third a distribution of objects. The first one does not differentiate between *pictura* and *littera*, because "it is necessary that the thing appertain to that without which it cannot subsist" (D.6.1.23.3–4). The second one is that of the *pretium* (ibid. and I.2.1.33–34). From the first two rationales, *superficies solo cedit* and *pretium*, the third one gives foundation to the opposition between writing and painting. Commentary writers multiply the forms of value, like Bartolo's prevalence of liquid over dry, even though the latter absorbs the former, or Alberico's reference to the multiple forms that affects sacred spaces.

Very early, gloss writers write about the "pretiosissima [. . .] pictura." Such is the case in two glosses from the *Digestus Vetus* regarding painting, attributed to Irnerius (early twelfth century) by Enrico Besta, which state in connection with D.6.1.23 that the *tabula* appertains to the painting "si pretiosissima sit pictura."[1] However, two other glosses edited by Paola Maffei exhibit the opposite opinion.[2] As for his famous disciples, while Bulgaro († 1166) and Iacopo († 1178) accept the *pretium* principle for painting, only Martinus († ca. 1166) applies it, for the first time, to writing. If letters are more precious than the support, then the latter is absorbed and must appertain to the writing:

Bulgarus et Iacobus dissentiunt in literis, licet aureis, positis in aliena charta vel membrana; nam sine distinctione dicunt cedere chartis. Martinus contra; ait enim ita demum cedere chartis, si chartae sunt pretiosiores, et hoc adserit argumentum tabularum.

[Bulgaro and Iacopo do not agree about the letters one draws on a *charta* or a parchment that belongs to another, even if gold; in fact, they assert without distinguishing that the letters appertain to the *chartae*. Martino, on the contrary, states that they appertain to the *chartae* only when the *chartae* are more precious, and in this, he adopts the argument of the tablets.][3]

Thus, the concept of *pretiositas*, mentioned in Irnerius's first glosses, now finds itself at the heart of the debate on painting, and also on writing, as the gloss writers adopt the quote "propter pretium picturae" from the *Digest* (6.1.23.3) and the "vilissimae tabulae" from the *Institutes* (2.1.34). However, *pretiositas* does not always belong to the same order. We saw that, for Placentin, one of its forms is that of *dignitas*. However, Azo and Accursio, in his Great Gloss, ignore that distinction and *pretiositas* belongs to both the order of price and that of aesthetic value—provided aesthetic value is understood as precise craftsmanship and use of proper colors, which, in fact, brings us back to value.

This is confirmed in Cennini's *Libro dell'arte*. The author advises the painter to always use the finest gold and good colors, particularly to paint Our Lady's figure, even if the patron cannot pay for them and the painter will earn little; because if he does so, his reputation will be such that he will earn rich patrons. The price of pigments, gold leaves, and gems that adorn the pictures is thus fundamental.[4] Cennini hardly mentions *compositio* or *historia*; he is not interested in the rhetorical structure of the painting, whereas Alberti makes it the center of the debate; planes are gathered into limbs, limbs into bodies, and bodies into the coherent scenes of a narrative painting.[5] No such concern in Cennini or Theophilus. It is not "painting Ulysses in such a way that one realizes his madness is not real but feigned and a pretense"[6] that gives the work its value.

The value of colors is both that of their cost and that of their hierarchy as envisaged by medieval culture and philosophy, full of a mysticism of the Dionysian-inspired light that gives value to all that shines.[7] In a treatise that will draw the most violent insults from Lorenzo Valla, *De insigniis et armis*, Bartolo spells out this hierarchy.[8] For the commentary writer, colors are more or less noble either according to what they represent—gilding represents sunlight; *purpureus seu igneus* represented the fire element and the second source of light; *asureus*, the air, which is transparent and *corpus dyaphanum*—or according to what they are *in se*, in which case one can regard white as the noblest, because it is closer to light, and black as the least noble, in that it is closer to darkness.[9]

Another text, belonging to a completely different genre, the *Opticae* by the Polish monk Witelo, which draws from the work of Ibn al-Haytham,[10] also informs us on how to understand the concept of *pulchritudo*. The word is not used by jurists, but the text provides a sense of how a completed work was valued. First, it must be noted that contrary to the tradition of ancient optics—which regarded the elements of the visible as light, color, position, form, size, and movement—Ibn al-Haytham enumerates other *visibilia*: light and color, distance, position, volume, form, size, discontinuity and continuity, number, movement and rest, beauty and ugliness, resemblance and dissemblance.[11] This nomenclature thus includes all operations that relate to appreciation and comprehension in the realm of the visible.

First, light and color produce this "placentia animae, quae pulchritudo dicitur" (the desire to please the soul one calls beauty).[12] However, there is also—and Witelo then uses painting and writing as examples—the *lineatio decens* (the harmony of the drawing) and the *ordinatio partium venusta* (the elegant arrangement of the parts), the size, the place, and certain features of the bodies that Witelo accepts as the result of the *consuetudo*, which produce that sense of beauty.

In pluribus tamen istorum consuetudo facit pulchritudinem: unde unaquaeque gens hominum approbat suae consuetudinis formam, sicut illud, quod per se aestimat pulchrum in fine pulchritudinis: alios enim colores et proportiones partium corporis humani et picturarum approbat Maurus, et alios Danus, et inter haec extrema et ipsis proxima Germanus approbat medios colores et corporis proceritates et mores: et sicut uniquique suus proprius mos est, sic et propria aestimatio pulchritudinis accidit uniquique.

[However, it is more often from the familiarity with those figures that beauty derives. It follows that each human nation appreciates the form with which it is familiar: in a way, it believes that what it regards as beautiful is the ultimate beauty. Indeed, a Moor and a Dane appreciate different colors and proportions in pictorial representations of human anatomy; and between those two extremes and their confines, the German appreciates intermediary colors, body dimensions, and customs; and just as each has a particular way of life, each has a particular notion of beauty.] (p. 185)

Quoniam plures intentiones non uidentur pulchrae, nisi per ordinationem partium et situum: unde scriptura et pictura, omnesque intentiones uisibiles ordinatae et permutatae non apparent pulchrae nisi per comptentum sibi situm: quamuis enim figurae literarum sint omnes per se bene dispositae et pulchrae, si tamen una ipsarum est magna et alia parua, non iudicabit uisus pulchras scripturas, quae sunt ex illis.

[Since a fairly large number of *intentiones* seem beautiful only due to the place and ordering of their parts, writing, painting, and all the ordered visible *intentiones* whose regularity has been upset seem beautiful only if one disregards their place. Indeed, even if, taken individually, the figured letters are all beautiful and laid out well, let one small letter abut a large one, and the eye will not find the resulting writing beautiful.] (p. 186)

The word *intentio* is used in the *De perspectiva* treatises of the thirteenth century as equivalent to *species* in the following sense: all visible objects generate or "multiply" *species* of light and color in the adjacent transparent milieu, which in turn generate more. These visible *species* transmit the accidents of the object to the eye that is looking and upon which, in a way, they are "imprinted."[13] Roger Bacon (ca. 1220–92), whose work influences John Pecham's and Witelo's, offers the following words as being synonymous with *species*: *virtus, similitudo, ydolum, simulacrum, fantasma, forma, intentio, passio, impressio,* and *umbra philosophorum.*[14]

Thus, the criteria for *pretium* in Azo and in the great Accursian gloss are the cost of materials and "aesthetic value," but only in the sense that was discussed above, that is, light and color effects, proportion, and arrangement of the parts.

Besides, Azo refers to Placentin as if, for him, *pretium* represented the reason for the *praevalentia* of painting, leaving aside Placentin's efforts to distinguish between *pretium* and *dignitas.* Azo was also the first to pick up Martino's idea of assimilating writing to painting because of its value, which led him to state that the support appertains to the writing, a statement hardly possible in the Justinian text. For Azo, "the scribes of our times have become painters," and writing, therefore, is always more valuable than the support.[15]

The idea of writing as art will be developed by Odofredo, who, independently of the material used, defines it as the art of form drawing, of the beauty of letter shapes, and, of course, of the contents, which he alone will evoke briefly in relation to sacred writings, "formerly" subject to the same principle as any other writing: they appertain to their support. Odofredo goes as far as reversing the proposition by stating that the *scriptores* of his day are the painters of yesteryear, and the painters of his day are the *scriptores* of yore, because they are much less accomplished than the great artists of the past. He gives two examples of the "*mala littera*" of the ancients: the copy of the *Pandectas* found in Constantinople and kept in Pisa, and the gold, but almost "vilest," letters of an emperor's will, which can be seen in Ravenna.[16] Furthermore, he was the first to attribute the promotion of the art of writing to the development of the universities.[17] For him, writing is once and for all tied to the principle "charta cedit scripturae" (the *charta* appertains to the writing), and it is painting that falls under the conditions that prevent systematic appurtenance to the support. The technical ability of the painters of his days, he states, is not sufficient to dictate a systematic rule, and, as for Placentin, price boils down to the idea of *dignitas* based on the subject represented and the use of precious colors. Odofredo's text probably is the most adamant about regarding the subjects of the representation as an argument for value. He also distinguishes between painting and writing in a way that assimilates writing to the art of drawing, of pure forms, and of lines, independently of the substance used, as opposed to painting, the dignity of which derives from technical ability, value of the pigments, certainly impact of the colors,[18] and mostly the subject represented, even though the painters of his days cannot compete with those of yore. Writing remains a formal value beyond its content, beyond what it "represents"; no theme seems to inhabit the movement of the lines. No other author will insist as much on its dignity.

Bartolo also develops the idea of *pretium*, only to reject it as a criterion to distinguish between painting and writing. For him, the rationale that must govern the debate is entirely different. Indeed, it is the relationship between liquid and dry things, and the whole and the part are envisaged in terms of area coverage. If one is to believe Bartolo, Rainiero da Forlì's interpretation is wrong, because, as we have seen, he inverts the principle governing the *media sententia*.[19] Besides, for him, painting and writing respond to the rationale of the part and the whole in terms of coverage, and if *littera cedit charta* (writing appertains to the *charta*), whereas on the contrary *tabula cedit picturae* (the *tabula* appertains to the painting), the reason is that "writing does not cover all in the way that painting covers the entire *tabula.*"[20]

Pars cedit toti et liquidum cedit arido, si ei uniatur [. . .] non enim pretiosius trahit ad se: imo charta, quae est arida, trahit ad se liquidum. Unde ratio pretiositatis nihil ad factum. Unde ratio est, quam ponit hic Iuriscunsultus, scilicet quia sine eo, cui cedit, esse non potest. Differentiam inter literam et picturam dixi in d. § literae. Nam scriptura non occupat totum sicut pictura occupat totam tabulam.

[The part appertains to the whole and what is liquid appertains to what is dry, if it is united to it. (. . .) Indeed, what is more precious does not attract: on the contrary, the *charta*, which is dry, attracts the liquid. Whence the valid argument is not the *pretiositas*, but that which the jurisconsult establishes, namely that it cannot subsist without that to which it appertains. I dealt with the difference between letter and painting in d. § *literae* (D.41.1.9.1). Indeed, writing does not cover the whole in the way that painting covers the entire board.]

Therefore, *pretiositas* is not the price but a value defining the nature of substances according to their hierarchy in creation. A liquid, whatever it may be, is more "precious" than something dry, and the principle of *pretiositas* as price cannot govern the relationship between liquid and dry substances. The sole reason for the difference between writing and painting is that no writing covers the totality of the support, whereas painting does. This difference is neither based on the rationale of *specificatio*, for which Bartolo criticizes Rainiero's usage, nor on the fact that painting would create a new *species*, exceeding the *tabula*, to which it could not be reduced; this difference is based on the fact that painting occupies the entire surface, covers it without any blanks, continuously, whereas writing, even when dense, always retains blank spaces between its signs.

However, such rejection of value as a criterion explaining the status of painting is infrequent. The authors generally try to account for the *preciosa pictura*, which Justinian discusses forcefully. Johannes Faber's commentary to the *Institutes* also shows us another interpretation of the *pretium*. For him, if the *pictura-tabula* relationship is governed by *pretium*, then what is the meaning of it? He points to the greater rarity of painting, probably both as an object and as an instance of a more complex technique. It is more common to write than to paint; writing is of more daily and ordinary use, and as such it is less precious than painting. Painting on *tabula* is governed by the price, now understood as rarity of the objects and degree of technical achievement.

Scriptura pretiosior esse potest et charior quadam pictura. Quid enim si modica imago pingeretur de carbonibus vel de nigro atramento: vel econtra: litere de auro. videtur quod membrana cederet literis et tamen constat de contrario [. . .] Quid ergo si tabula sit de cypresso vel cedro que sunt pretiose et pingatur de carbone vel alio vili colore. Videtur contra per dictam rationem. sed potest dicere quod cum in constitutione iuris non attendantur que raro sed que frequenter fiunt [. . .] et raro contingat quod pretiosa tabula pingatur vili colore sed econtra. vilis tabula colore nobili quod semper tabula cedat picture [. . .] et esset secus si statua etiam lignea pingeretur vel paries etiam ligneus: quia pictura cederet materie cum non derogetur rationi Pauli nisi in tabula tantum [. . .] vnde si pictura fieret in membranis sicut tota die fit de pincello. crederetur quod cederet charte vel membrane [. . .] Quid ergo si scriberetur in tabula forte dealbata [. . .] semper starem rationi Pauli quod scriptura cederet tabule quamuis secus in pictura: nam vt plurimum pictura esset difficilior et pretiosior quam scriptura. ante enim scripsisses vnum folium papyri quam aliquis pictor pinxerit imaginem quantuncumque modicam. et picture vt plurimum fiunt de coloribus pretiosis: et iura adaptantur ad ea quae frequenter etc.

[Writing can be more precious and costlier than a painting. In effect, what of a mediocre image painted in charcoal or black ink, or on the contrary, of gold letters? Parchment should obviously appertain to the letters, and yet the opposite prevails. (. . .) And what if a tablet of cypress or cedar wood, which are precious woods, were painted in charcoal or in another cheap color? The opposite would obviously apply, due to the aforementioned reason. However, one can say that, as in a legal text, only frequent and not rare occurrences are considered, and it rarely happens that a precious tablet is painted in a cheap color (rather, the opposite is true), accordingly a cheap tablet appertains to a valuable color, because the tablet always appertains to the painting (. . .) Yet, it would be different if a statue or a wall were painted: the painting would appertain to the support, because the reason given by Paul is invalidated only in the case of a board (. . .). It follows that a painting on parchment, as is done every day by brush, would appertain, one would think, to the paper or parchment. (. . .) And what if one wrote on a fortuitously whitened board? (. . .) I will always uphold Paul's reasoning, which makes the writing appertain to the board, even though it is otherwise for paintings, because painting, he states, more often is more difficult and more precious than writing. In fact, you could cover an entire page of paper with writing before a painter could paint a single image, even a mediocre one, and paintings are most often done in precious colors. Besides, the law responds to frequent occurrences, etc.][21]

However, a second element deserves attention: the manner of focusing the interpretation on the strict meaning of the word *tabula* as a wooden board, while it is most often used generically to designate the support for a painting. Indeed, he states that only a painting on *tabula* is capable of incorporating its support. For him, the paint is absorbed, not only by the wall, which is normal, but also by the parchment and the *charta*, which would mean that all illuminations must appertain to the parchment or paper that supports them. There is a double explanation for this rule that makes the illuminations disappear into their support. Not only parchment or paper prevails over paint, of any kind, but if the painting, even one done on a *tabula*, is meant to adorn a text on that same wooden board, then it must take the path of the adorned thing and, like the letters it adorns, be absorbed by the *tabula*. It is, therefore, as ornament to a text—which is always incorporated into its support—that illuminations lose their legal individuality.

Quid ergo si principio tabule sit pictura in primo loco: et scriptura postea sequatur. Videtur quod tunc pictura cedat tabule: quia illa pictura fuit apposita gratia ornandi literam: et sic cedit tabule vt scriptura.

[What if the painting is applied to the tablet first, and the writing after? It seems that, in such a case, the painting appertains to the tablet, because that paint was applied only to highlight a letter: under those conditions, it appertains to the tablet, like writing.]

The theme of *pretiositas* recurs like a quasi-systematic argument applied either to painting or to writing. However, it is important to remember two facts. On the one hand, the words *pretium* and *pretiositas* do not always designate the same thing. They may apply to the price of the substances applied or to their support, as well as to the value of the art and technique of writing and painting; or to the rarity of the painted objects relative to writing, once writing has become a more common practice. However, they may also apply to the subject of the representation, to a hierarchy of the things of creation, or to the respective value of sacred and nonsacred things; since, when Alberico[22] defends Placentin's opinion that "the thing of greater price must attract that of lesser price," he relies on Gregory IX's *Decretals* and Bonifacius VIII's *Sextus*, which state that the sacred attracts what is not.[23]

On the other hand, at least in medieval times, the criterion of *pretium* does not necessarily imply the creation of a new *species*, as Francesco Lucrezi claims about the classical and postclassical eras. Indeed, if the value of a painting, and for some that of the letters drawn on papyrus or parchment, could mean that the painted or written object composed of a support and an addition to it had become a new *species*—that the work and the substances applied to the support transformed its original form, so that it was impossible to distinguish between them, and that the new *species* could not be reduced to its original material—there is also a second way of approaching *pretium*, by which what is added to the support does not fuse with it to create a new *species*. Writing and painting can thus be united to their support without necessarily becoming one with it. If painting can be conceived of as the layer of colors forming an image independent from its support, writing can be similarly conceived of as the ink or any other material that traces forms on a surface, that is, two things which, while being practically inseparable nonetheless remain two and do not become a new third one. The value would then be that of those theoretical layers of paint and writing, which would prevail over the support without implying a new *species*. In that case, the element bringing painting and writing closer to the rationale of *specificatio* was their proximity to *ferruminatio*—the fact they are governed by the mode of junction of one substance by the same substance, by a physics of molecules that produce a unified body, containing *uno spiritu, una elementatione*, the gloss will state, even if, as we have seen, this rationale of *ferruminatio* was not necessary either.

Chapter 9
The Part and the Whole

According to Roman law, the *pars* is considered that which, in relation to the whole, is an element whose subtraction would make the thing seem mutilated, diminished in its essence, in its integrity.[1] Thus one regards the painted *tabulae* set into the walls and marble incrustations (D.19.1.17.3) as *partes* of the house, but not the wood panels that surround the walls or drapes (D.19.1.17.4). The mast is part of the boat, but not the prow's sail (D.50.16.242). Similarly, the lead used in the roof of a house is *pars*, but not that used to cover an uncovered terrace (D.50.16.242.2).

In the ordinary glosses, the *pars* permits one to ascertain the relations between things that are *factae*, as well as between things that are *infectae*. An arm that is attached to a statue is considered *pars*, and so is raw silver mixed into another and that is transformed into a mass made up of two parts that remain indivisible within the *dominium* of each original owner.

Item loquitur hic quando factum facto argento iungitur: et fit eius pars. Vbi autem infectum infecto, quilibet suae partis dominus permanet.

[One speaks similarly when raw silver is mixed with smithed silver: it becomes a part of it. However, when one mixes raw silver into raw silver, each remains the owner of his own part.] (D.6.1.23.2 *Adiecerit*)

This is the first criterion and the only relevant one to think about the mix of two things that are *infectae* found in a common mass.

On the contrary, the word *pars* appears to have two meanings when applied to things that are *factae*. It can connote a part endowed with a form, specificity, or name, such as an arm, a handle, or a foot; but it can also designate a part, one might say, without a name, to which only the categories of *minor* and *maior* can be applied.

Sed vbi factum facto, ita quod neutrum alteri cedit vt pars: dic quod minus maiori cedit. si neutra maior, cedit pretiosiori. si autem nullum pretiosius, tunc nullum alteri.

[But when one joins one *facta* (substance) to another *facta* (substance), since thus neither is subordinate to the other as a part, you must say that the smaller appertains to the greater. If one is not greater than the other, the less valuable appertains to the other. And if neither is more valuable than the other, then neither appertains to the other.]

In any case, the *accessio* will be irreversible only if the adjunction is performed through *ferruminatio*. The ordinary gloss of D.6.1.23 proposes a series of successive criteria to assess the *accessio*, which are organized in the following manner. The first opposition is between things that are *infecta* and those that are *facta*. If the relationship is between things that are *factae,* one decides based on the relationship between the part and the whole in its first form, the one that implies a definite form, or a name; otherwise, one judges based on the definition of the parts as *maior* and *minor* and the mode of adjunction: *ferruminatio* or *adplumbatio*. This series can be found in Azo's *Summa,* and it is quite systematically applied.

However, it is mostly in the fourteenth century that the rationale of the part and the whole becomes widely promoted through the categories of scholasticism. In his commentary to the *Digest,* Baldus affirms that the smaller part appertains to the greater,[2] and refers to the three modes of interpretation of the part and the whole that Bartolo developed about D.32.89. The whole and the part, says Bartolo, can be understood in diverse ways, either as a *universale* whole and a *subiectiva seu predicamentalis* part—this is the relation of *species* to *genus,* such as that between the animal *genus* and the "partes subiectivae seu praedicamentales" which would be the human or cattle *species.*[3] Or as an *integrale* whole and a *pars integralis*—just as an estate is an integral whole that can be divided into integral parts such as usufruct and ownership; and so, when a part is removed the whole is incomplete. Or, finally, as an integral whole and a share, such as a quarter, a third, and so on.[4] Furthermore we know that, for Bartolo, the *tabula* appertained to the painted work whereas the writing appertained to the *charta* as a minor *pars* insofar as the writing did not occupy the entire surface of the *charta,* wheras the painting occupied the entire *tabula.* One can suppose, therefore, that the *pars* Bartolo speaks of for writing and painting is the *pars integralis.*[5]

This tripartite division is common among authors of the fourteenth and fifteenth centuries and corresponds to categories that belong to logic. In reality, however, discourses about the *pars* and the *totum* proliferate and exhibit considerable diversity. The nonorthodox *partes* under consideration may have been created by the jurists themselves, probably from adjectives, although some can also be found in metaphysics and physics texts that exhibit true inventiveness on the subject of *partes*.[6]

In his famous *Dictionarium iuris*, Alberico de Rosate addresses the traditional tripartite division between *pars integralis, subiectiva* and the use of shares—half, quarter, third, and so on.

Pars aliquando sumitur pro qualicunque parte siue dimidia siue tertia siue alia dummodo non intelligatur de toto [...] Sed tunc potius dicitur portio quam pars. cum non sit conuertibilis pars enim semper convertitur.

[One sometimes admits that a "part" should be defined as being any part of a whole— a half, a third, or other—as long as it is not identified with the whole. (...) But then it is best to speak of "portion" rather than "part," since it is not convertible. In fact a part can always be converted.][7]

This convertibility of the part into the whole, often expressed in formulae such as "in toto enim pars continetur" (the whole always contains the part, D.2.14.27 *In decem prodesse*) or "qui agnoscit partem, videtur agnoscere totum" (he who acknowledges the part, obviously acknowledges the whole, Bartolo da Sassoferrato, *In secundam Infortiati*, D.31.60), is not, however, systematic. One can see, for example, in Jason of Mayno's commentaries,[8] a sort of part meaning, on the contrary, that which is hardly indispensable to the whole, and which may perhaps be regarded as *accidentalis*: a part which is neither *substantialis*, nor *essentialis*, nor *praedicamentalis*, nor *subiectiua*, nor *integralis*. This is the case of legacies, for example, in a will.

Pars dicatur est, sine qua totum consistere possit. nam dies est pars stipulationis ... et tamen stipulatio potest consistere absque die ... Sed ad hoc respondet d. Alex. [...] quod dies est pars qualitatiua, non autem pars substantialis, vt no. Bar. [...] sed praedicta loquuntur de parte substantiali. Concludo igitur, quod legata non sunt pars substantialis, nec essentialis testamenti, nec praedicamentalis, nec subiectiua, nec est integralis, sed bene sunt pars accidentalis, cum possint adesse, et abesse propter corruptionem subiecti, et sic testamenti.

[One calls a "part" that without which a whole can still exist: for example, the date is part of a stipulation ... and yet a stipulation can exist in the absence of a date ... But *dominus* Alex (Alexander Tartagni of Imola) responds (...) that a date is a qualitative part, and not a substantial part, as stipulated by Bartolo (...) but the topic of the substantial part was discussed above. From this I concluded therefore that legacies do not constitute a substantial or essential part of a will, nor a *praedicamentalis, subjectiva*, or integral part, but, rather, an accidental part, since they may be present or absent as the result of an alteration of the substratum, that is to say of the will.][9]

Now let us return to Alberico. In one of his glosses to the word *pars*, he proposes a series of categories that could not be subsumed within the previous three. There is, he says, the *pars continens* whose example is that of the womb, since the *venter* of the mother also designates that which it contains; the *partus*, the child to be born, who is "mulieris portio … vel viscerum" before the birth.[10] There is the *pars informans*, such as the color of the skin for mankind. The example given for the *pars adornans* is that of the testicles;[11] for *pars similitudinaria*, the usufruct;[12] for the *pars constitutiva*, he cites the hands; for the *pars inclusiva*, the key and lock; for the *pars inhaerens*, the serfs tied to the cultivated land.[13] It must be pointed out that none of these categories (*continens, informans, similitudinaria, inclusiva, inhaerens*) existed in classical Roman law.

Where the *tabula picta* is concerned, the vocabulary related to the *pars* is used in the *Summa Institutionum "Iustiniani est in hoc opere,"* edited by Pierre Legendre,[14] a work which, according to André Gouron, was probably written around the year 1127, in the Valence area, under martinian influence.[15] The author says that only an apparent contradiction exists in the text of the *Institutes* I.2.1.26:

Set quod in instit. dicit quod uestimentum preciosiorem purpuram ad se trahit contrarium uidetur d. lib. vi. ubi dicit quod prevalentior pars trahit ad se alteram, ueluti de pictura et tabula. Solutio. Si quis recto animo inspexerit nullum uidebit contrarium quia in inst. dicit cum pars coniungitur toto et totum trahit ad se partem, ueluti uestimentum trahit ad se purpuram, in dig. uero loquitur in eo casu cum pars coniungitur parti utraque simul iuncta faciunt totum ut ex pictura et tabula fit imago. Tunc enim prevalencior pars trahit ad se alteram et iterum sic potes obicere. Quamuis in eo casu pars coniungitur toto ita fit ut dicis tamen in eo casu cum pars iungitur parti tue diffinitioni contradicere uidetur liber instit., uidelicet cum dicit edifitium quodcumque sit solo cedere uel litteras cartis licet auree sint. Solutio. Vere solum est pars domus et carta pars libri et trahit ad se preualentiorem partem quod ideo contingit quia accidit ei rei sine qua esse non potest, set pictura potest esse sine tabula ueluti in muris. Edifitium uero sine solo, scriptura sine carta esse non potest. Et si quis huic nostre diccioni contradictor existat, uidelicet dicendo scriptura in tabulis posse fieri vel in alia materia, ita respondeatur. Nam ad ea pocius debet aptari ius que frequenter et sepe contingunt quam ad ea que raro accidunt.

[But the *Institutes*, which say that a piece of clothing, even if less valuable than purple, attracts it, seems in contradiction with Book 6 of the *Digeste*, that says that the part that has the greater value attracts the other, as in the case of the painting and the tablet. The solution: if one undertakes a rigorous examination, one will see that there is no contradiction, because the *Institutes* say that when a part is united with the whole, the whole attracts the part, as the piece of clothing attracts purple, while in the *Digeste* the case in question is that of a part united with a part, the junction of the two thereby permitting the formation of a whole, just as the painting and the tablet permit the formation of the image. So, it is in fact the part that has more value that attracts the other. And thus you can make a second objection: in the case where a part is united with a whole, it is truly as you say; however, in the case where a part is united with another part, the book of the *Institutes* is in manifest contradiction with your definition: it is evident at once when it says that a building, whatever it is, is subordinate to the land or that letters, even gold ones, are subordinate to the *chartae*. The solution: that is right, the land is a part of the house, the *charta* is a part of the book, and these parts attract to themselves parts that are more valuable: this is because a part finds itself subordinate to an element without which it cannot exist. But paint can exist without a tablet, for example on walls, while a building cannot exist without the land, nor writing without a *charta*. And if an opponent should argue against the point we have just made, declaring, naturally, that writing can be found on tablets or on another material, one should answer that law must respond to common and current cases rather than to rare instances.][16]

This last statement is manifestly false if one thinks about the importance of tablets in writing practices and their link to the verb *dictare* (to compose), which must be distinguished from *scribere* (transcribe). The reasoning is awkward insofar as the question is not really of precise hypothetical support but, rather, of the relationship between a particular and actual support, and that which has later been added to it in a specific case. But in any case it confirms this possibility that a painting can be thought of in the abstract, without the base upon which it is inscribed, as opposed to a writing, which is always inscribed on a substratum.

Chapter 10

Ornandi Causa

Another criterion must be added to the previously mentioned plurality governing the union or transformation of materials, which, in turn, cancels the rules of inseparability, part, and price: the *ornandi causa*, whose consequence is that *ornamentum sequitur rem ornatam*. The gloss and commentary writers refer generally to Title 34.2 of the *Digest* dealing with gold and silver legacies, and particularly to D.34.2.19 *Cum aurum*. Let us first review the texts in question:

Perueniamus ad gemmas inclusas argento auroque. Et ait Sabinus, auro argentove cedere. Ei enim cedit, cuius maior est species, quod recte expressit Semper enim cum quaerimus, quid cui cedat: illud spectamus, quid cuius rei ornandae causa adhibetur: ut cessio accedat principali. Cedant igitur gemmae phialis uel lancibus, inclusae auro argentove.

[Let us now turn to gems set in silver or gold. Sabinus says they appertain to the gold or silver, because an element appertains to the other whose *species* is more important. He is right to so affirm. Indeed, each time we ask which element appertains to which, we assess which was added to ornament the other, so that the accessory appertains to the principal. Gems must therefore appertain to the vessels or spears when they are set in gold or silver.] (D.34.2.19.13)

In margaritis quoque et auro idem est. Nam si margaritae auro ornandi gratia adhibitae sunt, auro cedunt. Si contra, aurum margaritis cedet.

[The same goes for pearls and gold. Indeed, if pearls have been added to embellish a gold object, they appertain to the gold. If the situation is reversed, the gold appertains to the pearls.] (D.34.2.19.15)

Idem in gemmis annulis inclusis.

[The same [applies to] gems set in rings.] (D.34.2.19.16)

Siue gemmae sint in aureis vasis, siue in argenteis, auro argentove cedant: quoniam hoc spectamus, quae res cuius rei ornandae causa fuerit adhibita, non quae sit pretiosior.

[If gems are on gold vessels or on silver vessels, they appertain to the gold or silver, because we assess which element was added to embellish the other, and not which is the most precious.] (D.34.2.19.20)

Once one has established which of the two elements is the ornament of which, regardless of the respective price, one assumes, as the ordinary gloss prescribes, that, by means of a legal fiction, there is extinction of the added ornament. Indeed, the excerpt "cuius maior est species" (D.34.2.19.13) seemed to call for a commentary, and the gloss explains it applies neither to price nor to quantity. Contardo Ferrini's interpretation of *species* as the set of characteristics of a thing—what makes that thing specific—clarifies both the syntagma and the gloss, which bring *ornandi causa* closer to *specificatio*.

Non pretio vel quantitate: sed ornandi vel specificandi causa posita [...] Et sic fictione iuris dicitur gemma extingui, et non possederi si autem neutrum alterius causa apponatur neutrum alteri cedit, et vtrumque possidetur.

[Not by its price or its quantity, but when it is used to embellish or specify (...) And thus, by way of a legal fiction, one says that there is (legal) extinction of the gem, and it cannot be owned. However, if none of the two elements was added to embellish the other, none appertains to the other, and one and the other can be owned.] (D.34.2.19.13 *Species*)

The ornament seems to abide by both the principle of *accessio* and that of *specificatio*, to the extent that it generates a new object. As such, it contradicts the rule of *praevalentia* and shatters its rationale. Such was also Bartolo's opinion. For him, gold should appertain to the gem if the gold was "*causa gemmae,*" and vice versa, but the *causa* could be extrinsic to the relationship between the materials composing that object; hence a ring made "causa ornandi mulierem" (to adorn a woman), or a seal ring in which "argentum poneretur causa gemmae" (silver is used to hold the gem) due to its utility.[1]

For Paolo da Castro, the *ornandi causa* must be a primary criterion permitting one to determine whether the *tabula* appertains to the painting:

Interdum pictura fit ad ornatum tabulae, et ipsius tabulae gratia, ut in cameris dominorum, ubi pinguntur postes de uili materia ad ipsorum ornatum, et tunc pictura cedit tabulae [...] aut econtra, tabula adiicitur gratia picturae, et tunc aut est uilis pictura, et idem dici potest, ut hic [...]. Aut est pretiosa, et tunc econtra, tabula cedit picturae, ut in contrario, et quae fit ratio differentiae inter picturam, et scripturam. dic, ut ibi notatur.

[Painting is sometimes meant to embellish a tablet, for the sole benefit of the tablet, as in noblemen's rooms, where the door jambs are painted with a material of little value to embellish them: painting then appertains to the tablet (. . .) or, on the contrary, the tablet is added for the benefit of the painting, and then one of two things occurs: either the painting has little value and the same can be said here (the painting appertains to the tablet) (. . .) or the painting is valuable, and the opposite applies: the support appertains to the painting, because the situation is reversed. This is the reason for the difference between painting and writing. You must make pronouncements according to these guidelines.][2]

According to Alberico,[3] the ornament criterion cancels the opposition between *ferruminatio* and *adplumbatio*, because if one considers that the adjunction was made *ornandi causa*, one must not hold on to the rationale of the mode of junction between the materials and the *species*, since "ibi loquatur de iis, quae ad ornatum pertinent" (this deals with [he refers to D.34.2. Si non sint § peruen.] that which relates to the embellishment), to things that are added "rei perfectionem" (to perfect the thing).

However, to my knowledge, the most extraordinary text about *ornandi causa*, which incidentally bears on the issue of *tabula picta*, is a commentary to the *Institutes* by Jacobo de Belviso,[4] related by Alberico. The concept of ornament is tackled by Alberico with the vocabulary of accessoriness, as it should.[5] About *Perueniamus*, he will discuss the *tabula picta* while reflecting on the principle "accessorium sequitur principale." Is accessory, he states, "cuius est maior species.i. cuius gratia adhibetur" (this is about that which concerns embellishment).[6] Then, he says, while referring to a gloss by Oldrado da Ponte Laude,[7] what should one make of the paintings that, once applied, disappear into the specified things? Jacobo de Belviso gave another interpretation of the same: the *tabula* appertains to the painting because it gives it form and beauty ("dat formam et pulchritudinem tabulae") in the same way that sex "in quo praeualet, dat ei formam et esse, et ipsum disponit in illud esse, propter praeualentiam sexus" (has more value than what it endows with form and identity, and it constitutes the very identity of the body on which it is, due to its superior value); thus value becomes irrelevant since, otherwise, a greater value should be allocated to male or female, when in fact the question is a different one: "et ideo inspicitur, quod plus est, et non quod pretiosius, quia masculus et foemina ordinantur et cognoscuntur per sexum" (and if one pays attention, which is better, it is not because one is more precious than the other, but because male and female organize and recognize themselves by their sex). Thus, starting from a discussion of the accessory and the ornamental, Alberico arrives at a definition of the status of the *tabula picta* in which the support disappears and explains it by analogy with the concept of sex as the element giving form and being to an indistinct body.

Chapter 11
Qualitas *and* Substantia

In his commentary at D.6.1.23, Angelo de Ubaldi (1328–ca. 1407), Baldus's brother, both categorizes the relationship between *substantia* and *substantia,* and reflects on the relationship between *substantia* and *qualitas* focused on painting and writing. Paint and writing, which are both applied on their respective support, are of the order of *qualitas,* whereas the *tabula* and *charta* are *substantiae,* and *qualitas* "*per se non potest.*" For him, the *praevalentia* is a criterion based on the *qualitas-substantia* relationship; and the *substantia* always prevails over the *qualitas,* which depends on it.

Quandoque qualitas adiungitur substantie. Exemplum in pictura que imponitur tabule et scriptura que imponitur carte [...] qualitas semper cedit substantie cum sine ea esse non possit unde scriptura carte et pictura tabule.

[When the quality is united to the substance. Example: when paint is applied to a tablet and writing to a *charta* (...) the quality always appertains to the substance, because it cannot exist without the latter. Consequently, writing appertains to the *charta,* and painting to the tablet.][1]

The criterion of *pretiositas* may, nonetheless, correct that rule by giving prevalence to the costliest; and for that reason, he opines that the *tabula* may appertain to the painting based on the price, and only if this condition is verified (except when the painting is done on a wall, in which case the painting appertains to the wall, which in effect constitutes an undisputable rule): "Et attende quia non erit idem in pictura muri nunquam enim talis pictura trahit substantiam ad se propter suam preualentiam" (And note that the same will follow for a mural: never does a painting of that kind attract a substance due to its superior value).[2]

However, it is also interesting to review the categories from which painting and writing are excluded, since many of the cited examples were used by other authors to discuss, on the contrary, the issue of the *tabula picta.* There are, says

Angelo de Ubaldi, seven types of *portio*. The first one, the *portio quottitatiua* or *quantitatiua*, designates the respective share of common property two persons retain when they commingle their wheat or one's silver with the other's gold into a common mass, with a double caveat: that the resulting body be not separable and that there be no *specificatio*, that is provided the mixed *species* remain "within a same substance and *species*" (D.6.1.5.2 *Vtraque*).

The second category is the *integralis*, the absence of which prevents one from regarding a body as having integrity. The examples are those relating to the statue regarded as one body made of several integral parts contained *una elementatione* and to the *tignum iunctum*. Looking back on the tripartition proposed by Bartolo, we are reminded that writing and painting fell under the category of *pars integralis*; however Angelo does not resort to that category to discuss the *tabula picta*.

The third category is that of the *portio subiectiva uel predicamentalis*, since when one speaks of the whole, one understands one speaks of the whole as *genus* and of that part as *species;* such as, for example, when one speaks of a yew versus the whole flock, or of the people or the legion. That part "non cohaeret corpori ymo distat et per consequens non efficitur eius cuius est corpus per agregationem sed remanet eius cuius erat" (is not connected to the body; it is, on the contrary, separate from it, and consequently it does not revert to the owner of the body formed by aggregation: it remains the property of he who previously owned it); this category refers us to the third type of bodies under Pomponius's definition of tripartition in D.41.3.30, that which the medieval jurists call *universitas rerum*.

The fourth category is the one he names *ordinamentalis*.[3] The example is that of the gem set in a ring. When the gem is *introclusa*, the two elements constitute a single body, although not under the regimen of *portio quottitatiua*, because they belong to different *speciei*; nor under that of *portio predicamentalis* to the extent that there is no *genus-species* relationship; nor yet under the rationale of *pars integralis*, because each part has integrity and this is why it is named *portio integralis*. In reality, the example will be later discussed under the ornament rationale: if the ring was made to adorn the gem, then it must appertain to the gem. Some authors retained this category of the ornament to explain the prevalence of painting over *tabula*, but Angelo does not.

The fifth category is a variation of the second (*integralis*): namely, *formalis*, the absence of which renders the object deformed. Indeed, one may regard one part as *integralis et formalis*, such as the arm of a statue, which affects its form, and another part as *integralis sed non formalis*, such as the *tignum iunctum*, the absence of which does not deform the house.

The sixth category is the *portio qualitatiua*: "per dictam adiunctionem corpus totale qualificatur" (said adjunction bestows quality to the whole body). For example, as to fruits and plants that are one with the land, one may say they constitute a *portio qualitatiua*, since when they are present the land is regarded as better and costlier, and when removed, it becomes *uilior et deterior*: this type of part always appertains to the body on which it is dependent.

The seventh and final category is that of the *portio intextualis*. It is conceived of in relationship with that form of *accessio* generated by *alluvionem*, namely that of drifting trees, of land chunks carried by the river, by the ebbing of the river which increases the landmass of the riverbank owner before nature claims it:

Et per aluuionem possimus forsitan dicere quod sit septima et ultima portio que appellatur intextualis. Exemplum si linea margaritarum aut etiam fila aurea uel argentea intextuetur in uestimentis ut fieri uidemus cottidie.

[And perhaps we could mention alluvium to speak of the seventh and last portion, namely *intextualis*. Example: a row of pearls or gold or silver threads woven in garments, such as we see daily.]

The added thing retains its individuality to the extent that it can be separated. The example is odd. On the one hand, no author had proposed that alluvium could include things added through human intervention. For Azo, alluvium was the very example, along with progeny, of *accessio divina*; and, within this category, the example most remote from the effects of the river flow, is Azo's fruition metaphor to illustrate the *incrementum latens*, namely secret and imperceptible growth. On the other hand, the idea that *alluvio* could be separate from what it appertains to is foreign to its status. Nothing, except perhaps the idea of an *accessio continua* (meaning continuous in the spatial sense) could account for the analogy.

So that, for Angelo, the relationship between *portiones* or *partes* and the whole can only be conceived of under a substance-to-substance rationale; those categories are based neither on the principle of pure attraction, which make plants appertain to the land they feed from; nor on the transformation or production of a new *species*. It is nonetheless true that those categories do not originally entail systematic procedural consequences, as was the case for rules such as *superficies solo cedit* or *pars cedit toto si ei uniatur*. In fact, this classification intersects with practically all the previously mentioned ones and still does not order the procedures any differently. By leaving aside the painting and writing issue, by positing it as a relationship between *qualitas* and *substantia*, by distancing it from the trees, the beams, the statues, the pearls, the fruits, and the ornaments, Angelo seem to account for its strangeness, for the impossibility of reducing it to systematic opposites that would permit the ordering of things in successive categories. Painting and writing seem to resist abiding fully by any rule, inscribed in a "soil" from which they derive no food, impossible to separate while being, for all that, a single body, parts of a part. This is particularly true of painting since, as Johannes de Platea will write, it reverses all principles. It is an artifice stronger than matter, a substance carried away by accident, and a liquid that absorbs the dry.

Littere etiam si auree sunt cedunt chartis et artificium seu opera cedunt materie: et qualitas seu accidens substantie. et liquidum cedit arido. sed in pictura est totum econtra. quia tabula cedit picture: et sic substantia cedit qualitati et accidenti: et aridum cedit liquido.

[The letters, even if gold, appertain to the *chartae*; the craftsmanship or labor appertains to the material; similarly, the quality or accident appertains to the substance, and the liquid to the dry. However, in the case of painting, there exists a complete inversion, since the tablet appertains to the painting, and consequently it is the substance that appertains to the quality and accident, and the dry to the liquid.][4]

Conclusion

To order the interpretations, let us return first to the *Summae*, which were elaborated between the second third of the twelfth century and the beginning of the thirteenth century. Under Placentin's construction, the *accessio* subsumes the *specificatio*. The main split is between things that are separate, always discussed in terms of "birth" and for which he uses the verb *accedere*, and things that are continuous in the spatial sense, but deprived of birth, for which he uses *cedere*. Birth designates fruits of the womb, islands, *species*—among which painting under certain conditions—whereas *accessio continua* includes seeds and plants of another that grow on my field and, generally, all that is ruled by the principle *superficies solo cedit*—among which writing; things joined, inset, and encased; *alluvio* as an imperceptible increase; and construction timber. This classification may appear paradoxical if one considers it should be governed by a conception of birth dominated by a nature that gives life to plants, trees, and wheat, in the same way it gives life to animals and humans. However, for Placentin, birth is defined by separation, and in that sense, a tree cannot legally be born because it lives only if its roots anchor it into the soil from which it gets nourishment. Yet to list painting among the things that are born and writing among those that are not, did introduce a new element previously foreign to this principle of classification. At issue was the image as representation and also as presence; and one could evoke here what Jean-Claude Bonne calls the *thingness* of the image ("choséité de l'image"), that is, not an evocation of the sacred via the iconic or stylistic quality of the images, but the immanence of the sacred in the "substantiveness" of the image.[1]

For Azo, who organizes his discussion around *accessio* based on the principle of the agent (God, Man, both), the distinction between what was born separate and what grows or is added to a continuity concerns only the *accessio* generated by God, that is, the opposition between fruits of the womb and *alluvio*. What really matters is his way of discarding the value of things from the moment God intervenes as a sole or partial agent: as in the first category (fruits of the womb and *alluvio*), in the third (where the agents are God and Man) regarding plants and wheat, as well as trees, value does not permit allocation of the ownership of the things. Only the second category—that of *accessiones*, the agent of which is human intervention (*ferruminatio, adplumbatio, tignum iunctum, insertis, intextis, inclusis, aedificatio, pictura,* and *scriptura*)— permits a rationale based on value. If the principle of agency is not systematically retained, the implicit value structure thus proposed will, on the contrary, dominate.

The *specificatio* as one criterion influencing the discussion on painting emerged in the schools of the French Midi. Placentin mentions this, and so does the *Summa Iustitiani est in hoc opere*. The Provençal schools that developed during the twelfth century exhibit an interest for the liberal arts that Azo and Accursio criticize, as they extol the self-sufficiency of the law. Azo's acerbic discourse on Placentin's "fables" regarding the creation of the new *species* are reminiscent of his scorn for Bernando Dorna's flowery speeches, a front for his attacks against the Montpellier master.[2] Odofredo—who, like his master Iacopo Balduini, stands for an alternative to Azo's and Accursio's scholastic currents, which were dominant in Bologna—exploits the same theme. The first generation of Orléans masters will also attend Balduini's school, which explains the prestige of Odofredo's *lectura* among Orleans scholars. The use of the *specificatio* argument can thus be explained as a school-specific phenomenon of little following, because it conflicted with the "mainstream" of Bologna authors, who associated painting with *accessio* only.

From the twelfth century, the criterion of value—which the Romans accepted for painting only—finds support for writing as well. However, this argument, disseminated during the thirteenth and the beginning of the fourteenth centuries, is refuted by Bartolo. Even though he was not always followed, the recognition of his work thus signals a return to the primary rationale under which painting and writing must abide by the rule *superficies solo cedit*. According to Bartolo, the *tabula picta* must remain closer to the trees and sowed plants, and to river alluvium—as occupied area—than to "artificial" things defined in the *Tractatus de fluminibus* by their final cause—the house is made to be occupied, the vessel to be drunk from.[3] This is, therefore, a return to the original forms of *dominium* acquisition. This does not mean that the concepts of labor or value are absent from his rationale, but they need not be invoked in the present context.

The fundamental Justinian opposition between value and soil attraction remains the primary structure. However, medieval authors rephrase it as an opposition between a material-based rationale and a value-based rationale. Only value, it seems, may break away from the successive oppositions developed in discussions of materials and things. When one moves away from the criteria based on things that are added or mutated, toward things that are *ferruminatae, factae,* or *infectae,* value is invoked. Without being univocal, it operates as if it had no opposite. It is not a term of dichotomy, because the alternative "value/of little value" is not expressed and is even explicitly rejected in some cases, such as Placentin's. The recurrence of value indicates that Yan Thomas's propositions for the classical Roman period on the value of a thing being the thing itself must be taken into account in order to understand the rationales specific to the Middle Ages, provided, however, that one remains attentive to the meanings attributed to the value of things and remembers that medieval authors developed an important discourse on matter and things, even when, in the final analysis, they often chose value. The rules of procedure show that the value issue systematically appears in judiciary rules under the form of compensation offered to the party that does not obtain the thing litigated; but it also appears as an intrinsic rationale in the very definition of things.

This value rationale is not necessarily linked to that of *specificatio,* as Francesco Lucrezi proposed for classical and postclassical Roman law. Value does not appear because there is production of a new thing. Authors who never mention *specificatio* mention the category of value almost systematically in connection with painting and frequently in connection with writing. Therefore, value is not connected to creation per se. Placentin's and Odofredo's notions of *specificatio* rest as much on creation, understood as the use of a technique, as on *dignitas,* in the sense of the majesty of the image. For them, painting does not raise the issue of the creation of a new, specific thing, whatever it may be. Rather, it is about conceiving an object of majesty. Besides, those very same authors will speak of the value of writing, which no one envisages in terms of *specificatio.*

In his dissertation, Laurent Pfister[4] holds that the concept of an author's rights emerged from the specific way Christianity approached the connection between the creation of a work and *dominium* by granting only to God the act and power of creating. This divine privilege occupies a preeminent place in the *dominium Dei* thesis.[5] The world belongs to God, God is the world's *dominus,* because God created the world. Progressively approached as a right, *ius,* over all things created, the *dominus Dei* thesis would be the model for an author's property right over his or her creation. However, this model is the fruit of a very long history, and one should not read such a conclusion in texts that do not assume it. The issue of writing as content, as creation, as immaterial thing, is never raised by the *ius commune* jurists of the classical era. Nor is the issue of creation clearly raised for painting, at least where painting is understood as an ineffable thing, beyond materiality. The jurists do not equate *ars*, or *manus pretio*, with what we conventionally call "art."

This also leads us to a discussion on the relationship between painting and writing in the Middle Ages. Writing is made of nonmimetic visual signs. The monastery scribes of the late Middle Ages gave a symbolic interpretation to letters, whose shape perpetually evoked the Christian universe; but even though a particular reference could be associated with each letter—the cross in "x"; both Testaments in the two *virgulae* in "B"; or the Trinity in the three legs of "m"[6] —their sequence was devoid of any intrinsic meaning. The promotion of calligraphy from the thirteenth century on accompanies an exaltation of the art of drawing free from systematic symbolic evocation. The metaphors of writing as painting, and the value jurists assign to it from the end of the twelfth century on, make it possible for writing to change the principle by which it should always appertain to its support and invert the principle that organized the hierarchy between writing and image in the West. The "Gregorian model," which subordinates images to writing,[7] is inverted by jurists who reject an image modeled on language, used to demonstrate and narrate what cannot be read, and endorse writing as modeled on pictorial forms. This inversion is possible precisely because the issue of painting and writing in the *tabula picta* is approached outside of any rationale of representation or meaning. For the same reason, Azo makes fun of Placentin when he proposes an approach to *specificatio* based on what painting represents, because the master from Montpellier introduces a referential criterion in concepts that must be envisaged along a rationale of acts and substances devoid of any mimetic function. Painting and writing must be held as gestures comparable to hunting or sowing.

In discussing materials and *species*, I tried to show the diversity of interpretation jurists could tap from, starting from a small number of elements or, rather, forced to revert to a small number of solutions. To return to the world of things, to speak in one way or another of material notions, is not just to see or touch or know what an object is made of or the concrete forms of its manufacture and use, far from it—even though these are fundamental issues. It also means to know how one reasoned about materiality, which is a way of naming and ordering the experience of the senses. The legal doctrine is particularly loquacious on materiality issues; to ignore it and focus only on a judicial practice one endows with more reality is, in my opinion, a poor way of thinking of the real. The plurality of the rationales does not, however, imply arbitrariness. If matter is not the ultimate explanation or the limit of interpretation, the discourse nevertheless mentions land, trees, river waters, wooden boards, a world of things subjected to codified forms and rigorous categories. Thus, to say that, for the Middle Ages, the issue of the *tabula picta* essentially is a textbook case in no way diminishes its importance; textbook cases may help elucidate the "architectures of the mind" brilliantly evoked by Jean-Pierre Vernant. In order to understand the *tabula picta*, one must restore it in the series of things that are odd to us, where it belongs: things that are born, like humans, animals, islands; things that cannot subsist without their land, like buildings, plants, or seeds; things that are added, like ornaments such as purple, gold threads, or rows of pearl woven into a cloth; the quality of a substance; and the sex of a body. Writing and painting—which modern thinking defines as a separate and disincarnate world removed from the material rationales applicable to manufactured, sold, and consumed goods—have been durably described using the categories permitting things to be ordered and reflected upon. Our encounter with the reasoning of medieval jurists has attempted to revive this common allegiance.

Appendixes

1. D.41.1.7.7–8: *Gaius, libro secundo*

Rerum cottidianarum siue aureorum

7. Cum quis ex aliena materia speciem aliquam suo nomine fecerit: Nerva et Proculus putant hunc dominum esse qui fecerit: quia quod factum est, antea nullius fuerit. Sabinus et Cassius magis naturalem putant rationem efficere: ut qui materiae dominus fuerat, idem eius quoque quod ex eadem materia factum sit: dominus esset: quia sine materia nulla species effici posset: veluti si ex auro vel argento vel aere tuo aliqua fecero vasa: vel ex tabulis tuis navem aut armarium aut subsellia fecero: vel ex lana tua vestimentum: vel ex vino et melle tuo mulsum: vel ex medicamentis tuis emplastrum, aut collyrium: vel ex uvis tuis aut olivis aut ex spicis tuis vinum vel oleum vel frumentum. Est tamen etiam media sententia recte existimantium: si species ad eandem materiam reuerti possit: verius esse quod et Sabinus et Cassius senserunt: quod si non possit reuerti, verius esse quod Nerua et Proculo placuit: vt ecce vas conflatum, ad rudem massam auri vel argenti vel aeris reuerti potest: ac nec mulsum quidem ad mel et vinum, vel emplastrum, aut collyria ad medicamenta reuerti possunt. Videntur tamen mihi recte quidem dixisse, non debere dubitari: quin ex alienis spicis excussum frumentum eius sit, cuius et spicae fuerint. Cum enim grana quae spicis continentur perfectam habent suam speciem: qui excussit spicas, non novam speciem facit, sed eam quae est detegit.

8. Voluntas duorum dominorum miscentium materias, commune totum corpus efficit: siue eiusdem generis sint materiae: veluti vina miscuerunt, vel argentum conflauerunt: siue diuersae: veluti si alius vinum contulerit: alius mel: vel alius aurum, alius argentum: quamuis mulsi, vel electri noui corporis sit species.

[7. A man who has produced a *species* for himself from a substance not belonging to him is regarded as its owner by Nerva and Proculus, because, they say, the product previously belonged to no one. According to Sabinus and

Cassius, natural reason rather commands that the owner of the substance also be the owner of what is produced from it, because without matter, no *species* can be produced thus in cases where with your gold, silver, or bronze I make vases; with your planks, a boat, a wardrobe, or benches; with your wool, a garment; with your wine and honey, honey wine; with your medicines, a plaster or a collyrium; with your grapes, olives, or seeds, wine, oil, or wheat. Nevertheless, there also exists an intermediate position: some consider with reason that if the *species* can revert to the same substance, the fairer judgment is that of Sabinus and Cassius; if it is impossible, the better counsel is that of Nerva and Proculus: thus, if melted, a vase may revert to a shapeless mass of gold, silver, or bronze. By contrast, wine, oil, or wheat cannot revert to grapes, olives, or seeds; and honey wine cannot revert to honey and wine, nor the plaster or the collyrium to medicines. In my opinion, however, one is right to affirm that, without a doubt, wheat extracted by threshing the harvest of another belongs to the owner of the harvest. Indeed, when the grains from the harvest have their final *species*, he who threshes the harvest does not produce a new *species*, but only brings to light one that already existed.

8. Two owners who decide to mix materials make a whole body owned by both in common, be it with materials of the same type—for example if they mixed wines or melted silver—or of a different type—for example if one brought wine and the other honey, or one brought gold and the other silver—and whatever the *species* of the new body, honey wine or *electrum*.]

2. D.32.52 *Ulpianus, libro vicesimoquarto ad Sabinum*

Pr. Librorum appellatione continentur omnia volumina, siue in charta, siue in membrana sint: siue in quauis alia materia. Sed et si in philyra: aut in tilia ut nonnulli conficiunt: aut in quo alio corio idem erit dicendum. Quod si in codicibus sint membraneis: vel chartaceis vel etiam eboreis: vel alterius materiae vel inceratis codicillis an debeantur, videamus. Et Gaius Cassius scribit, deberi et membranas libris legatis. Consequenter igitur caetera quoque debebuntur si non aduersetur voluntas testatoris. [...]

4. Quod tamen Cassius de membranis puris scriptis verum est: nam nec chartae purae debentur, libris legatis nec chartis legatis libri debebuntur: nisi forte ad hoc nos vrserit voluntas: ut puta si quis forte chartas sic reliquerit, Chartas meas universas qui nihil aliud quam libros habebat, studiosus studioso. nemo enim dubitabit, libros deberi nam et in vsu plerique libros char-

tas appellant. Quid igitur si quis chartas legauerit puras? Membranae non continebuntur: neque caeterae ad scribendum materiae.

5. Sed nec coepti libri scribi. vnde non male quaeritur si libri legati sint, an contineantur nondum perscripti. et non puto contineri: non magis quam vestis appellatione nondum detexta continentur: sed perscripti libri nondum malleati, vel ornati continebuntur: proinde et nondum conglutinati vel emendati continebuntur: sed et membranae nondum consutae continebuntur.

6. Chartis legatis, neque papirum ad chartas paratum neque chartae nondum perfectae continebuntur.

[Under the name "book," we include all manuscript rolls, be they made of papyrus, parchment, or any other material. However, even when they are made of linden or reed,[1] as made by some, or of any other membrane, they will be referred to by the same name. And if it relates to parchment *codices*, papyrus, even ivory,[2] or another material, or even small wax tablets, let us see if they are owed. Gaius Cassius also writes that parchments are also owed when the books are part of a legacy. From this it follows that all the rest will also be owed, unless the testator's will runs contrary to this. (. . .)

4. However, what Cassius writes about blank parchments is correct. Indeed, blank *chartae* are not owed when the legacy is for books; and if the legacy is only for *chartae*, books are not owed, except when under certain circumstances an express will so constrains us: for example, if someone willed his *chartae* with the following language "all my *chartae* without exception." For someone who owned only books, (a legacy) from a scholar to a scholar: none will question that the books are owed. In fact, most people are in the habit of calling *chartae* "books." What then if someone willed blank *chartae*? Parchments and other writing supports shall not be included.

5. However books whose writing is only begun will not be either. It follows that it is not incongruous to review whether, in the case of book legacies, incompletely written books are included. And in my opinion, they are not, just like the word "garment" does not include unfinished cloth. But fully written books that have not yet been hammered or adorned will be included, and so will those whose sheets have not been glued or corrected,[3] as well as parchments not yet sewed together.

6. When the legacy is for *chartae*, one will include neither papyrus that has not yet been prepared to make *chartae*, nor unfinished *chartae*.]

3. Odofredo, *Interpretatio in vndecim primos pandectarum libros*, Lyon, 1550: *Sed et id quod* (D.6.1.23.3)

Potest ita dici ibi in veritate scriptura cedit charte. sed tabula picture non pictura tabule. [...] Sed iterum dicet aliquis pro deo que est ratio diuersitatis quare scriptura cedit cartis. pictura vero non tabule. Ratio assignari potest: et potest videri manifeste maxime in regijs vrbibus rome et constantino. olim tempore harum legum homines nesciebant scribere. vnde scriptura cedebat cartis: siue essent sacre scripture de incausto vel de auro. vnde si videatis pandectam que est pisis que pandecta quando constitutiones nostre fuerunt facte fuit deportata de constan. pisis est de mala litera si videatis literas aureas que olim fiebant quasi vilissime sint sicut potest videri rauenne in testamento cuiusdam imperatoris scripto de literis aureis. vnde scritura cedit cartis: sed olim optimi fuerunt pictores. vt in regijs vrbibus potest videri ita sciebant antiqui pingere vix moderni attingerent pedem eorum. vnde olim tabula cedebat picture: et hoc tangit literam licet de pictura quidam contra senserint propter precium picture: habetis ergo que scriptura cedit carte: olim quia vilior carta est preciosior quam scriptura et vilius cedit preciosiori. vt.infra. de aur.et ar.le.l.et si non sint.§.perueniamus. (D.34.2.19.13) sed quid dicemus hodie scriptores nostri temporis effecti sunt pictores. pictores nostri temporis facti sunt scriptores propter alteratum ingenium hominum grates scholaribus: preciosior est scriptura quam carta. dicemus hodie econtra propter alteram industriam et operam quod carta cedat scripture. In tabula dicemus sicut.infra. subijciam: si preciosor est tabula quam pictura. pictura cedat tabule. et econtra.et hoc dixerunt Io. et Azo. vel potest dici secundo modo sic pro tempore huius.§.indubitanter scriptura cedebat carte. hoc hodie immutatum non est: sed pictura cedebat tabule. hodie immutatum est. vt in.l.contra. quia non est nouum etc. supra de le. et sena.con.l.non est. (D.1.3.26) vel potest ita distingui si scriptura cedit carte et si aurea sit: quia preciossior erat olim carta quam scriptura. in pictura et tabula refert: aut tabula est dignior pictura tunc pictura cedit tabule et econtra. et hoc scripsit dominus Pla. elegantibus verbis in summa de re.di. (I.2.1) quod dicit.l. que tabula cedit picture intelligo verum esse si pingitur homo non sit bos vel vrsus. si pingitur de egregio colore non autem de calce. vnde noluit distinguere sic. si in tabula pingitur homo vel imago beate marie virginis et de bono colore de auro vel azurio tabula cedit picture. vt.in.l.contra sed si pingeretur de vili materia vt faciunt ultramontani pingunt limacem in vituperium italicorum vel scorpiones in vituperium vltramontanorum in pariente de carbone: inconueniens esset quod paries cederet picture.

*   *   *

[One can truly affirm here that writing appertains to the *charta*. However, the tablet appertains to the painting, and not the painting to the tablet. (. . .) But, in turn, someone will ask before God the reason for this difference between writing, which appertains to the *chartae*, and painting, which does not appertain to the tablet. One can provide it: one can clearly see, and mostly in the imperial cities of Rome and Constantinople, that in past times, at the time of those laws, men could not write. It follows that the writing appertained to the *chartae*, be it Sacred Texts written in purple ink or gold. On this subject, if you could see the Pandects of Pisa, which were brought from Constantinople to Pisa when our laws were drafted: their letters are poorly drawn; or if you could see the gold letters they drew in the old days, they are so to speak worthless, as can be observed in Ravenna on an imperial will drafted in gold letters. It follows that writing appertains to the *chartae*. However, there were in the past excellent painters. Thus, one can observe in the ancient imperial cities that our forefathers were such good painters that modern painters can barely compete. It follows that the tablet appertained to the painting. The same also applies to letters, even though some are of a contrary opinion with respect to painting, due to its value. You thus know what kind of writing appertains to the *charta*: the ancient kind, because a valueless *charta* is more precious than writing, and because a valueless property appertains to a more precious property (D.34.2.19.13). However, we are going to state why the scribes of today have become painters. The scribes have become the painters of our times because the scholars have modified their talent: writing is more precious than the *charta*. We will say that, today, conversely, the *charta* must appertain to the writing due to a different application and practice. As for the tablet, here is what we shall say as I will expound below: if it is more precious than the painting, then the painting must appertain to the tablet and vice versa. That is what Azo and Iohannes said. In addition, one can even say that, with regard to the era in which that paragraph was written, writing undoubtedly appertained to the *charta*: this is not unchanged today; by contrast, painting appertained to the tablet: this is unchanged today (D.1.3.26). One can notably determine that, if writing appertains to the *charta* even when it is of gold, it is because in past times the *charta* was more precious than the writing. About painting and the tablet, one of two things: either the tablet is more valuable than the painting, and then the painting appertains to the tablet, or it is the opposite. However, Master Placentin wrote in flowery terms in his *Summa* (I.2.1) that the law demands that the tablet appertain to the painting: I perceive the truth of this affirmation if the painting represents a man, and not an ox or a bear, and if the color is remarkable, not if it is done in lime. But then he fails to specify if, when the painting on the tablet represents a man or the image of the Blessed Virgin Mary in noble colors, gold or blue, the board should appertain to the painting. For if it were a valueless painting, such as those of the *Ultramontani* who paint a slug in charcoal on a wall to fustigate the Italians, or scorpions to fustigate the *Ultramontani*, it would be incongruous that the wall should appertain to the painting.

4. Odofredo, *Praelectione in postremum Pandectarum Iustiniani Tomum, uulgo Digestum, Lyon*, 1552: *Litere quoque* (D.41.1.9.1)

Unde litere licet sint auree, cedunt charte, quum fiunt a vili scriptura, [. . .] Sed chartula cedit picture, quum pictura fit ab egregio pictore, vt hic: quia inconueniens esset quod pretiosa scriptura cederet vilissime tabule [. . .] vnde dixit dominus Placen. et ista scripsit, Tabula cedit picture, si pingitur homo, et non vrsus. Item si pingitur de optimis coloribus. Sed si scriberet, alias pingeret aliquis de carbone, vel de gypso lunacarij, [. . .] tabula non cedit picture. Unde dixit Placen. et ita scripsit, quod dicit ex tabulam cedere picture, verum est, si pingitur homo, non vrsus, vel aliquid simile. Unde si pinxit figuram domini nostri Jesu Christi, vel figuram sancte Marie, vel apostolorum, et facit optimis coloribus, tunc tabula cedit picture: secus si pingeret de carbone, vel de incausto, vel de aliquo alio vilissimo colore vrsum, vel limacem, vt faciunt Gallici quando volunt deridere Italicos. Idem est, si quis Italicus pingeret aliquem qui saporem pistaret, vel qui faceret salsam viridem. Et ita scripsit dominus Placen. in Summa sua [. . .] vt sit intentio sua quod pictura sit pretiosa ratione forme, vel conditionis [. . .] Secus si vili colore pingitur vrsus, vel limaca, vel aliquod aliud simile, vt in lege contraria. Et bene potest ita dici. Sed dominus Joan. et Azo inuiti sequebantur opinionem domini Placen. nec poterant ab eo deuitare. Unde inuidens dominus Azo domino Placen. scripsit talem doctrinam. Duo sunt tempora. Unum tempus est antiquum, quo fuerunt facte he leges. Aliud tempus est nouum, id est, presens tempus, in quo sumus nunc. Secundum antiquum tempus hoc est verum, quod litera cedit chartis, vel membranis: sed tabula cedit picture. Et est ratio, quia tempore homines non scripserunt, vel male, seu pessime scribebant: quasi secundum tempora harum legum magis essent pretiose charte, vel membrane, quam litere: sed tempore presenti inspecto, in quo simus nunc dicimus oppositum, scilicet quod charte cedant scripture: quia hodie scriptores non sunt scriptores, imo pictores: imo inspecto presenti tempore sunt pictores, non sunt scriptores: vnde dicimus quod charte cedunt literis. Et quod istud sit verum potestis videre in his libris Pandectarum [. . .]. In pictura econtra, quia olim summi erant pictores, quod potestis videre in statuis antiquis positis Rome, et Constantinopoli, quia hodie non inuenirentur tales pictores. Unde quia olim erat pretiosa pictura, et pretiosi pictores, tabule cedebant picture. Secus hodie, quia vilissimi sunt pictores.

[It follows that the letters, be they of gold, appertain to the *charta* when they are of poor penmanship. (. . .) But a part of the *charta* appertains to a painting when the painting is by an exceptional painter, since it would be incongruous that a valuable writing should appertain to a very cheap tablet. (. . .) Thus, Master Placentin states and writes as follows: "The tablet appertains to the painting if the painter has represented a man, and not a bear; and if he has used the best colors. But assuming a scribe or a painter used charcoal, stucco (. . .), the tablet does not appertain to the painting." From this, Placentin states and writes that the law says the tablet appertains to the painting; it is true if a man is painted and not a bear or some similar subject. It follows that, "if a painter has represented Our Lord Jesus Christ, the Virgin Mary, or the Apostles, and done so in the best colors, then the tablet appertains to the painting; it would be otherwise if he used charcoal, ink, or another very cheap color to paint a bear or a slug, as the French do when they want to make fun of the Italians. The same would apply if one painted an Italian grinding spices or cooking green sauce." Here is what Master Placentin writes in his *Summa* (. . .) so that his intent is that the value of a painting be a function of its image (*forma*) and its quality. The opposite applies if one paints a bear, a slug, or some other similar subject in a color of poor quality (. . .). And it is correct to so speak. However, Master Joannes and Master Azo reluctantly followed Master Placentin's opinion without being able to depart from it. As a result, Master Azo, dissenting from Master Placentin, wrote the following doctrine. "There are two eras. The first, which witnessed the emergence of those laws, is over. The other, more recent, is the current era, in which we now live. About the past era, it is correct that the letter appertain to the *chartae* or to the parchments; however, the tablet appertains to the painting. And the reason is that in those days men did not write or wrote poorly, badly even; as if during the years when those laws were made the *chartae* or the parchments had more value than the letters. By contrast, keen observation of the present era, in which we now live, makes us say the opposite, namely that the *chartae* appertain to the writing, because today the scribes are not so much scribes as painters. More: a keen observation of the present reveals that they are painters and not scribes. From this, we affirm the *chartae* appertain to the letters. And you can verify the truth of this affirmation in the books of Pandects. (...) As for painting, it is the opposite because in times past painters were fully eminent—as can be seen from the ancient statues in Rome or Constantinople—and one could not find such painters today. It follows that, since the painting of yesteryear was more valuable, since painters were worthier, the tablets appertained to the painting. It goes otherwise today because painters have become worthless."]

5. Alberico de Rosate, *In primam ff. Veter. Commentarij*, Venice, 1585: *Item quaecunque* (D.6.1.23.5)

Hic tanguntur duo modi coniungendi, unum cum altero. unius est per ferruminationem, alius per applumbaturam.est, et tertius, qui hic non tangitur, quem infra subijciam. primus ergo modus est per ferruminationem, nam per ferruminationem dicuntur coniungi quoties diuersa corpora eiusdem naturae, et speciei coniunguntur nulla alia materia mediante puta ferrum ferro, argentum argento, aurum auro, alia materia non mediante coniungitur, uel conflatur et idem in omnibus aliis metallis, quae sunt eiusdem naturae coniunguntur, uel simul conflantur, ut probatur in dic.l.quicquid. infra de acquerenda rerum dom. (D.41.1.27) et dicitur talis coniunctio, uel conflatio fieri per ferruminationem, quia saepius contingit talem coniunctionem, uel conflationem fieri in ferro, quam in alijs metallis. Idem tamen est, et alijs metallis, ut dixi. secundus modus est per applumbaturam, quod est quoties diuersa corpora eiusdem speciei, et naturae iunguntur mediante alia materia, quae non est eiusdem speciei, ut puta cum argentum argento iunguntur mediante plumbo, vel auro aurum, uel pannum cum panno, mediante filo. et ideo dicitur haec coniunctio per applumbaturam, quia per plumbum facilius et frequentius aliorum metallorum quam mediante alia materia, ut dicunt artifices. idem tamen, et si coniunguntur alia materia, quam plumbo, ut dixi in panno, quod coniungitur filo, et pariter in charta, et scriptura, quae coniunguntur mediante incausto, et tabula, et pictura mediantibus coloribus, ut statim dicam in § sed et id (D.6.1.23.3). Est, et tertius modus coniungendi quem uidemus saepe fieri per artifices, quia coniugunt materiam materiae per cauiculos paruos, quae coniunctio de facili potest separari, ut cum scypho pes adiungitur cum clauiculis eiusdem materiae. Et tunc, quia facilis est separatio credo agi posse ad exhibendum, ut separetur, et deinde agatur rei vendicatio. Et in primis duobus modis coniungendi est magna differentia, quia si iungo brachium tuae statuae meae statuae per ferruminationem efficior dominus totius, et partis vnde non potes agere ad brachium, nec statua durante, nec ea dissoluta, sed quia non est aequum, quod locupletetur cum iactura tua, ages actione in factum ad aestimationem brachij tui ferruminati. sed si iungo per applumbaturam, tunc donec statua durat non potes petere brachium, quia sum dominus totius statuae, sed petes aestimationem, sed ea dissoluta potes brachium uendicare. Sed contra praedicta opp. quod non debeat attendi facta coniunctio per ferruminationem, vel per applumbaturam, sed solum consideretur, cuius ornandi causa sit facta adiunctio, ut inf. de au. et arg. lega. l. et si non sint.§ perueniamus (D.34.2.19.13). Sol. ibi loquatur de ijs, quae ad ornatum pertinent, hic quando adiungitur rei perfectionem. Pro declaratione itaque omnium praedictorum distingue, cum quis coniungit materiam materiae, aut alienam infectam suae infectae, aut alienam factam suae factae, aut alienam factam suae infectae, aut alienae factae suam infectam. Quae autem dicatur facta, et infecta. supra declaraui in §.prox. praecedenti primo casu cum coniungitur infecta infectae puta alienam massam massae meae si quidem communi nomine, et uoluntate communi erit pro indiuiso et idem si casu fortuito sunt commixtae, uel coniunctae, ut infra de acquir. re.dom.l.adeo.§.uoluntas duorum. et Instit. de rer.di.§. si duorum.et duobus § seq. (D.41.1.7.8,I.2.1.27, 28 and 29) si autem suo nomine tantum coniungat alienam suae et volunte eius, cuius erat insolidum efficitur dominus, ut infra de acqu.re.do. (D.41.1.25) nisi uoluntate. Si uero suo nomine tamen, et sine voluntate eius, cuius erat si quidem facilis est separatio, ut quando iunctura est facta per applumbaturam quilibet remanet dominus. sicut erat pro parte diuisa, et uendicare poterit, quod suum est, ut infra de acqu. re.do. l.lacus.§.i.et l.in omnibus, et sic intelligatur in eo tit.l. quicquid.i.responso. (D.41.1.12.1, D.41.1.12.24 and 27) si autem sit difficilis separatio, ut quia iuncta est per ferruminationem, tunc massa efficitur communis, et quilibet vendicat dimidiam pro indiuiso, ut sup. eodem.l.2.§.fin. et l. seq. et l. idem Pomp. in prin.et probatur aperte, haec dist.ea.l. idem Pomponius § sed si plumbum. (D.41.1.27.2, D.6.1.5, D.6.1.5.2) Secundo casu quando coniungo alienam materiam factam meae factae, aut id, quod coniungo materiae meae factae est membrum, ut puta statuae tuam pedem, vel manum statuae meae adiungo: aut non est membrum, sed plus membro, puta pars dimidia, tertia, uel quarta. [. . .] Tertio casu principali quando tuam materiam factam adiungo meae infectae, vt puta scyphum tuum massae quilibet remanet dominus rei suae, sicut erat ante coniunctionem quocumque modo fuerit facta coniunctio, siue per ferruminationem, siue per applumaturam, et siue bona fide siue mala fide, cum facilis sit separatio, ut sup. eo.l.idem Pomponius. §.sed si plumbum

(D.6.1.5.2). Quarto casu principali quando tuae factae adiungo meam infectam; vt puta quando pingo in tabula tua, quae est materia facta, et pictura est
materia, tunc infecta, uel scribo in chartis tuis, uel pingo purpuram tuam. aut
mala fide, ut uideor donare, ut inf. de acq. re.domi.l.qua ratione. §.ex diverso.
et Instit. de re.diuis.§.ex diuerso (D.41.1.9, I.2.1.30). aut bona fide.et tunc aut
mea infecta est pretiosior tua facta, ut puta pictura pretiosior est tabula tua, si
bona fide facio totius nanciscor dominium. et si conuenior a domino tabulae
utili rei vend. repello eum doli expect. nisi mihi refundat expensas seu aestimationem picturae. Si vero mea infecta adiuncta factae est minus pretiosa,
quam facta cui adiungitur, vt litera adiuncta chartae, vel membranis ille est
dominus, cui est adiuncta materia minus pretiosa non ille, qui adiunxit. Sed
si dominus cartarum uendicet libros, repellitur doli mali excep. nisi reddat
aestimationem scripturae.

[Two ways of uniting a body to another are at issue here. The first one is *ferruminatio*, and the second, *applumbatura*. There is a third one that is not at
issue here: I will introduce it further down. Thus the first way is *ferruminatio*:
one speaks of union by *ferruminatio* when one unites different elements or
species of a same nature without the intervention of a different substance:
for example when iron and iron, silver and silver, gold and gold are united
or melted together without the intervention of another substance. The same
goes for all other metals of a same nature that are united or melted together,
as is shown in D.41.1.27. And one says that a union or fusion of this type
happens by *ferruminatio*, because such union or fusion happens more often
with iron than with other metals. However, one also uses the same word for
the other metals, as I said. The second way is *applumbatura*, which consists
in uniting diverse elements of a same *species* and of a same nature by means
of a substance different from that of the *species*: for example when one unites
silver to silver, or gold to gold, with lead, or fabric to fabric with thread. The
same goes for a *charta* and writing united by means of ink, and for a board
and painting united by means of colors, as I will soon state at D.6.1.23.3. There
is yet a third form of union, which we often see artists use: they unite one
substance to another by means of small nails; this makes for a union that can
be easily undone, such as when the base of a vessel is attached to it by a small
nail of the same material. Consequently, since the union is easy to undo, one
can, in my opinion, initiate an action *ad exhibendum* to undo the union, leading to a subsequent action in restitution. There is a great difference between
the first two modes of union, because if I unite the arm of your statue to my
statue by *ferruminatio*, I become the owner of the whole and the part. It fol-

lows that, by law, you cannot claim the arm while the statue is in existence, nor after the union is undone. However, since it is unjust that one should become enriched at your expense, you will initiate an action *in factum* to assess the value of the arm you contributed, joined by *ferruminatio*. By contrast, if I perform a union by *applumbatura*, you will not be able to reclaim the arm for as long as the statue subsists, because I am the owner of the whole statue; but you will claim payment. However, once the union is undone, you can claim the arm. Yet, I object to this, to the extent that one must not focus on the fact that the union was effected by *ferruminatio* or *applumbatura*, but only focus on what was added for ornamental reasons, as below D.34.2.19.13. Solution. Here one must speak of what pertains to adorning, as an addition to a finished object. This is why, considering all that was previously stated, you must, when someone has united one substance with another, distinguish between the union of another's substance that is *infecta* with his own substance that is *infecta*; another's substance that is *facta* with his own substance that is *facta*; another's substance that is *facta* with his own substance that is *infecta*; or another's substance that is *infecta* with his own substance that is *facta*. I explained above, in the previous paragraph, what is meant by *factum* and *infectum*. The first case is that of a substance that is *infecta* united to a substance that is *infecta*, for example the union of another's mass of gold to my mass of gold. If the union is truly realized in common and with common agreement, the common product shall be owned undivided. The same shall apply if the mix or union is accidental, D.41.1.7.8, I.2.1.27, 28 and 29. By contrast, let us suppose someone unilaterally unites another's substance to his own with the agreement of the former owner of the *insolidum* [matter that can be melted], he becomes the owner of the mix, as stated below at D.41.1.25, even if he does not agree. However, if the union was unilateral, but lacking the agreement of the former owner, and it is truly easy to undo, for example when the union is by *applumbatura*, one retains any ownership he had of the separable part and will be able to claim his property, as stated below at D.41.1.12.1, D.41.1.12.24 and 27. But if the union is hard to undo, for example because it was by *ferruminatio*, then the mass becomes common and each claims one undivided half, as in D.41.1.27.2, and D.6.1.5, and this is clearly demonstrated by D.6.1.5.2. The second case occurs when I unite another's substance that is *facta* to my own substance that is *facta*, or when what I unite to my substance that is *facta* is a limb, for example when I add to my statue a foot or a hand belonging to you: or it is not just a limb, but more, for example a half, a third, or a quarter of the object. (. . .) The third essential case is when I add your substance that is *facta* to my substance that is *infecta*, for example your vase with my mass:

each remains the owner of his property as before the union, no matter how the union was performed (by *ferruminatio*, by *applumbatura*, with or without good faith) because the union is easy to undo, as in D.6.1.5.2. The fourth essential case is when I add my substance that is *infecta* to your substance that is *facta*, for example when I paint on your tablet, which is a substance that is *facta*, whereas the paint is then a substance that is *infecta*; when I write on your *chartae*; or when I paint your garment with purple. Either I act in bad faith and it is as if I had given it, D.41.1.9, I.2.1.30, or I act in good faith and then one of two things: either my substance that is *infecta* is worth more than your substance that is *facta*, like paint being worth more than the tablet: if I act in good faith, I acquire ownership of the whole. And if the owner of the tablet sues me in an action for restitution, I resort to the fraud exception to rebut him, unless he reimburses what I spent or pays for my painting. However, if my substance that is *infecta* is worth less than a substance that is *facta* to which it was added, like letters added to a *charta* or to parchments, the owner is he who owns the substance to which a less valuable substance was added, and not he who performed the adding. But assuming the owner of the *chartae* claims the books, one resorts to the fraud exception to rebut him, unless he pays for the writing.]

Notes

Foreword

1. *Las verdades de los hechos. Juez, proceso y testimonios en la Castilla del siglo XIII* (Salamanca, 2004); "Savoirs féminins et construction de la vérité: Les femmes dans la prevue testimoniale en Castille au XIIIe siècle," *Crime, Histoire & Sociétés 2* (1999): 5–21; "Façons de croire: Le juge et les témoins dans l'oeuvre juridique d'Alphonse X le Sage, roi de Castille," *Annales, Histoire, Sciences sociales* (1999): 197–218; "Hombres frigidos, mujeres estrechas: La impotencia en el derecho canónico medieval," in Isabel Morant and Reyna Pastor (eds.), *Historia de las mujeres en España y América Latina*, tome I (Madrid, 2005), pp. 659–74, and, in collaboration with Ana Rodríguez López, "La recherché du vrai roi et la folie du juriste: Une double enquête dans le Compromiso de Caspe (1412)," in F. Bougard, J. Chiffoleau, and C. Gauvard (eds.), *L'enquête au Moyen Âge* (Rome, Paris, 2008).

Introduction

1. Armando Petrucci, "Dal libro unitario al libro miscellaneo," in Andrea Giardina (ed.), *Società e impero tardoantico*, vol. 4, *Tradizioni dei classici, transformasioni della cultura* (Bari, 1986), pp. 173–87.

2. Michel Foucault, "Qu'est-ce qu'un auteur?," *Bulletin de la Société française de philosophie* 64, no. 22 (July–September 1969): 73–104, reprinted in Daniel Defert and Françoise Ewald (eds.), with the collaboration of Jacques Lagrange, *Dits et écrits, 1954–1988* (Paris, 1994), vol. 1, pp. 789–821.

3. Mark Rose, *Authors and Owners: The Invention of Copyright* (Cambridge, Mass., 1993). See also Roger Chartier, "Figures de l'auteur," in *Culture écrite et société: L'ordre des livres (XIVᵉ–XVIIIᵉ siècle)* (Paris, 1996), pp. 45–80.

4. Michael Baxandall, *Giotto and the Orators: Humanist Observers of Painting in Italy and the Discovery of Pictorial Composition: 1350–1450* (Oxford, 1971).

5. Ibid., p. 47.

6. Ibid.

7. Ibid., p. 44.

8. About the first stages of the legal renaissance, see Ennio Cortese, *Il rinascimento giuridico medievale* (Rome, 1992). On the general history of the law in the Middle Ages, one may refer to the great synthesis by Francesco Calasso, *Medio Evo del diritto*: I. *Le fonti* (Milan, 1954), today surpassed only by Ennio Cortese, *Il diritto*

nella storia medievale, 2 vols. (Rome, 1995–96). On authors, one may refer to E. Cortese's book, as well as, more recently and including detailed bibliographies, Hermann Lange, *Römisches Recht im Mittelalter, Bd1, Die Glossatoren* (Munich, 1997).

9. Calasso, *Medio Evo del diritto*, p. 528.

10. *In primam ff. Veter. Part. Commentarij* (Venice, 1585).

11. One fundamental meaning should be discarded in this particular context: the term *species* does not refer to a class within the scheme *genus-species*. About this meaning in the work of Roman jurists, see Mario Talamanca, "Lo schema *genus species* nelle sistematiche dei giuristi romani," Colloquio italo-francese, Rome, April 14–17, 1973, *La filosofia greca e il diritto romano* (Rome, 1977), vol. 2. The term *species* is extraordinarily complex. For a sample of some of its meanings in the Middle Ages, see Pierre Michaud-Quantin, "Les champs sémantiques de *species*: Tradition latine et traduction du grec," in *Études sur le vocabulaire philosophique du Moyen-Âge*, in collaboration with Michel Lemoine (Rome, 1970), pp. 113–50.

12. In a fundamental article, Yan Thomas ("La valeur des choses," *Annales: Histoire, Sciences Sociales* [November–December 2002]: 1431–62) shows how the legal grasping of things in Roman law was not based on ontology but that, on the contrary, things had a specific status based on the constitution of their value as "arbitral value" grounded in common sense; and how the law called "thing" (*res*) a case, a trial, as well as the litigated thing. The thing is its price, value is its substance. This text was published too late to be truly accounted for in this book; but even if it displaces the nature of things in such a way that its implications for medieval law should be investigated, my question is that of the forms of materiality, which cannot dispense with the "physics" of things.

13. On *bona fides* giving rise to possession in Roman law, see Luigi Lombardi, *Dalla "fides" alla "bona fides"* (Milan, 1961), and in particular as to the commentators, pp. 208–49.

14. *Istituzioni di diritto romano*, reprint, Naples, 1974, p. 192 (2nd ed. rev. 1927), quoted by Francesco Lucrezi, *La* tabula picta *tra creatore e fruitore* (Naples, 1984), pp. 22 and 29.

15. So as not to overload the notes, I refer the reader to Lucrezi, *La* tabula picta, pp. 61–63, 79–126, and 250–66.

16. The theme of the *tabula picta* has also been tackled by the Romanists in connection with the issue of *specificatio*. One will find bibliographical indications in the chapter entitled "*Dominium* and Object Extinction," note 13.

17. Paola Maffei, *Tabula picta. Pittura e scrittura nel pensiero dei glossatori* (Milan: 1988). The author did an excellent work of editing. She also announced a future book on the commentators, which, to my knowledge, has unfortunately not been published.

18. Lucrezi, *La* tabula picta, p. 21, and P. Maffei, *Tabula picta*, p. 11.

19. Guillaume Durand (ca. 1230–96), *Rationale divinorum officiorum*, A. Davril O.B.S. and T. M. Thibodeau, eds. *Corpus Christianorum, Continuatio Mediaeualis*, 140 (Turnhout, 1995), lib. I, III, 4, p. 34.

20. Ibid. The bishop of Mende quotes Gregory the Great, *Regula pastoralis* II, 10: "Dum exteriorum rerum intrinsecus species attrahuntur, quasi in corde depingitur quicquid fictis ymaginibus deliberando cogitatur" (as the forms of the exterior ele-

ments are attracted toward the interior, the shaped images permit the mental representation of an object as if it were drawn in one's heart).

21. This is also true for Roman texts, Lucrezi, *La* tabula picta, pp. 22–23.

22. Quoted by Franck Soetemeer, "La carcerazione del copista," in *Livres et juristes au Moyen Âge* (Goldbach, 1999), p. 193, first published in *Rivista Internazionale di Diritto Comune* 6 (1991). About Odofredo, see Nino Tamassia, "Odofredo. Studio storico-giuridico," *Scritti di storia giuridica*, vol. 2 (Padua, 1967), pp. 335–464, first published in *Atti e Memorie Deputazione di Storia patria per la Romagna* (1894).

23. Rainiero de Perugia, *Ars notaria*, in Augusto Gaudenzi (ed.), *Scripta anecdota antiquissimorum glossatorum, Bibliotheca Iuridica Medii Aevi* II (Bologna, 1892), pp. 25–67, p. 60 as to the formula. There is no specific formula for painting.

24. Rolandino Passaggeri, *Summa totius artis notariae Rolandini Rodulphini Bononiensis viri praestantissimi eandem summam luculentissimus apparatus, qui Aurora per excellentiam dicitur . . .* (Venice, 1546), c. 120r, col. I.

25. Luciana Devoti, "Aspetti dell produzione del libro a Bologna: Il prezzo di copia del manoscritto giuridico tra XIII e XIV secolo," *Scrittura e civiltà* 18 (1994): 77–142.

26. Ibid., pp. 102–5. One can find numerous writing contracts executed in Bologna in Gianfranco Orlandelli, *Il libro a Bologna dal 1300 al 1330: Documenti con uno studio su il contratto di scrittura nella dottrina bolognesa* (Bologna, 1959), and also, for Bologna outside of the dates picked by G. Orlandelli, see the *Chartularium Studii Bononiensis: Documenti per la storia dell'Università di Bologna dalle origini sino al secolo XV* (Bologna, 1909–88), 15 vols.

27. Henri Denifle, "Die Statuten des Juristen-Universität Bologna vom J. 1317–1347, und deren Verhältniss zu jenen Paduas, Perugias, Florenz," *Archiv für Literatur und Kirchengeschichte des Mittelalters* 3 (1887): 196–493.

28. Leo Speluncanus, *Artis notariae tempestatis huius speculum* (Venice, 1575), fol. 221v–222v. Of course, the writing contracts also raise the issue of the *pecia* system, but we will not address it to the extent that it does not affect the goals of the present research.

29. About the existing penalties, see Soetemeer, "La carcerazione del copista." It may be a forced execution *(obligationes faciendi)* or the requirement of *id quod interest*; a gloss of Accursio about D.39.1.21.4 *Placuerit* gives the *actor* the choice, ibid., p. 202. However, this may also lead to the incarceration of the copyist. About this rule among the commentators, pp. 214 ff.

30. This is an apostil to the commentary to D.39.1.21.4 of Rainiero Arsendi da Forlì, *Lectura super digesto novo* (Lyon, 1563), reprint *Opera iuridica rariora*, vol. 9 (Bologna: 1968), quoted by Soetemeer, "La carcerazione del copista," p. 225. About Rainiero Arsendi da Forlì, see Ennio Cortese, *I diritto.*, vol. 2, pp. 426–27, n. 90.

31. About the importance of the commissioning party's requirements in the work of the Renaissance painters, see Michael Baxandall, "Les conditions du marché," in *L'Oeil du Quattrocento* (1972; reprint, Paris, 1985), pp. 9 ff.

32. Archivio di Stato de Palermo, 18 N, quoted by Geneviève Bresc-Bautier, *Artiste, patriciens et confrèries: Production et consommation de l'oeuvre d'art à Palerme et en Sicile occidentale (1348–1460)* (Rome, 1979), p. 206. One can find other commission contracts in Francesco Filippi and Guido Zucchini, *Miniatori e pittori a Bologna:*

Documenti dei secoli XIII e XIV (Florence, 1947), or in Gaetani Milanesi, *Documenti per la storia dell'arte senese* (Sienna, 1854), 3 vols., mostly vol. 1 regarding the thirteenth and fourteenth centuries.

33. About legal humanism, see Domenico Maffei, *Gli inizi dell'umanesimo giuridico* (Milan, 1956); Severino Capriolo, *Indagini sul Bolognini. Giurisprudenza e filologia nel quattrocento italiano* (Milan, 1969); Hans E. Troje, *Graeca leguntur: Die Aneignung des byzantinischen Rechts und die Entstehung eines humanisation "Corpus juris civilis" in der Jurisprudenz des 16. Jahrhunderts* (Cologne, 1971).

34. See the fundamental texts by Fernando Bouza Alvarez, *Corre manuscrito: Una historia cultural del Siglo de Oro* (Madrid, 2001), and by Harold Love, *The Culture and Commerce of Texts: Scribal Publication in Seventeenth-Century England* (Amherst, Mass., 1998).

35. Klaus Arnold, *Johannes Trithemius: In Praise of Scribes, De laude scriptorum* (Lawrence, 1974), quoted by Armando Petrucci, "Copisti e libri manoscritti dopo l'avvento della stampa," in Emma Condello and Giuseppe De Gregorio (eds.), *Scribi e colofoni: Le sottoscrizioni di copisti dalle origini all'avvento della stampa*, Atti del seminario di Erice. X Colloquio del Comité international de paléographie latine (October 23–28, 1993) (Spoleto, 1995), pp. 507–25, especially pp. 509–10.

Chapter 1

1. On the subject of Accursio, see Cortese, *Il diritto*, vol. 2, pp. 179–85.

2. I translate *pretium* sometimes as "price," sometimes as "value," in function of the context. When *pretium* refers to a sum assessed in a trial or when there is a sale or purchase, I translate it as "price"; in all other cases I translate it as "value."

3. I understand that there is no perfect identity between those verbs, as Paolo Maddalena aptly pointed out in "*Accedere* e *cedere* nelle fonti classiche," *Labeo* 17 (1971): 169–86.

4. Olivier Guyotjeannin, "Le vocabulaire de la diplomatique en latin médiéval," in Olga Weijirs (ed.), *Vocabulaire du livre et de l'écriture au Moyen Âge*, Actes, Paris, September 24–26, 1987 (Turnhout, 1989), pp. 126–27.

5. More likely than not, Accursio borrowed this gloss from his master's *apparatus*.

6. I.2.1.34 *Cedere*.

7. See in particular *La science du droit dans le midi de la France au Moyen Âge* [Variorum] (London, 1984).

8. On the subject of the method, see Peter Weimar, "Die legistische Literatur und die Methode des Rechtsunterrichts des Glossatorenzeit," *Ius commune* 2 (1969): 43–83, and more specifically, 47–50.

9. There is a large number of publications about Bartolo, among others, the studies collected in *Bartolo da Sassoferrato: Studi e documenti per il IV centenario*, Actes du colloque de Perugia, April 1–5, 1959, 2 vols. (Milan, 1962).

10. Baldus (1327–1400) studied in Perugia and taught in various cities until his death in Pavia. A famous commentator, the author of the *lecturae* to the *Digest, Codex,*

Decretales (interrupted at the beginning of Book 3, probably because of his death), and *Libri Feudorum*, he was also known for his *consilia*, a particularly profitable genre in which he was prolific. About Baldus, see Cortese, *Il diritto*, vol. 2, pp. 436–45, containing a thorough bibliography.

11. Cortese, *Il diritto*, vol. 2, p. 437 provides a bibliography about him, but in fact, little is known about Angelus de Ubaldi's life.

12. Giuseppe Branca, "Accessione," *Encyclopedia del diritto* (Milan, 1958), vol. 1, p. 261.

13. Here, I am following the definition given by Contardo Ferrini in "Appunti sulla dottrina della specificazione," *Opere*, vol. 4 (Milan, 1930), pp. 45–46. In the last years of the nineteenth century, *specificatio* was at the center of a lively debate between Romanists: see the bibliography in Waclaw Osuchowski, "Des études sur les modes d'acquisition de la propriété en droit romain: Recherche sur l'auteur de la théorie éclectique en matière de specification," in *Studi in onore di Vicenzo Arangio-Ruiz nel XLV anno del suo insegnamento,* vol. 3 (Milan, 1953), pp. 38–39. Ferrini's definition of *species* seems more adequate. Along with Contardo Ferrini's, the following works also deserve particular attention: Silvio Perozzi, "*Materia e species*" (1890), in *Scritti giuridici I. Proprietà e possesso* (Milan, 1948), pp. 226–52, and "Se la relazione sulle opinioni dei Sabiniani e dei Proculiani in D.41.1.7.7 sia di Gaio" (1890), in ibid., pp. 254–81; and Paul Sokolowski, *Die philosophie im Privatrecht* 1 (Halle, 1902). More recently, see Martin Josef Schermaier, *Materia. Beiträge der Naturphilosophie im klassischen römischen Recht* (Cologne, 1992).

14. Gianbattista Impallomeni, "Spezificazione," *Enciclopedia del diritto* (Milan, 1990), vol. 43, p. 267.

15. The Proculians belonged to the school of jurisconsult Cassius, who died under Nero, and the Sabinians to that of Sabinus, who died under Vespasian. See Jurist Paul's text (D.41.1.7.7–8) containing the opinion, defended by the Sabinians, dominated by the idea of a *naturalis ratio*, and the one, defended by the Proculians, supporting the *nova species* (see Appendix 1).

16. Such a comparison exceeds the bounds of the present project. In addition, it seemed to me, as I was studying the scholastic texts, that the lawyers' vocabulary and categories retain considerable autonomy. About *ferruminatio* and *adplumbatio*, I will nonetheless refer to Aristotle's concept of the "one" as seen by Saint Thomas. For example, see Averroes's commentaries to Book 2 of the *Physics* (*Aristotelis opera cum Averrois commentariis*, vol. 4, *De physico auditu* [Venice, 1562], fol. 50 ff.) and the *quaestiones* of William of Ockham (*Quaestiones in libros physicorum Aristotelis, Opera philosophica*, vol. 6 [New York, 1984], *Quaestiones* 118–22, pp. 116–29) and of Duns Scot (*In VIII libros physicorum Aristotelis quaestiones, Opera omnia*, vol. 2 [Paris, 1891], pp. 506 ff.).

17. Aegidius Romanus, *Egidii Romani commentaria in octo libros Physicorum Aristotelis*, 1502 (about Book 1, which addresses the necessity of a substrate, fol. 20v). The italicized section is the excerpt from Aristotle commented by Aegidius Romanus.

18. Lucrezi, *La* tabula picta, pp. 34–51.

19. Here I reproduce the translation provided by Yan Thomas, "La valeur," p. 1453, which takes the position that this text was incorrectly interpreted insofar as the meaning is not fundamentally that of the *specificatio*, but that of value as the substance of

the *res*, which appears clearly in the following excerpt: "quia videtur res ei abesse, cui pretium abest" (because a thing is assumed not to be there for him who has not the price of it).

20. See Appendix 2.

21. About the functions and the meaning of medieval images thought of within the framework of a "visual culture," see Jean-Claude Schmitt, *Le corps des images: Essai sur la culture visuelle au Moyen Âge* (Paris, 2002).

22. Jean Wirth, *L'image médiévale: Naissance et développements (VIᵉ–XVᵉ siècles)* (Paris, 1989), p. 268. The author works on the concept of *imago* as a phenomenon having a logical and semiological nature.

23. "Form that is without matter cannot be a subject, nor included in matter; it would no longer be a form, but an image. From those forms that are outside of matter derive those that are within matter and form the bodies, because they are images." Boecius, *De Trinitate PL* 64, col. 1250, trans. Jean Wirth, p. 80.

24. On the evolution of the relationship to images in the West, see Jean-Claude Schmitt, "De Nicée II à Thomas d'Aquin: L'émancipation de l'image religieuse en Occident," in *Le corps,* pp. 63–95, first published in François Boepsflug and Nicolas Lossky (eds.), *Nicée II, 787–1987* (Paris, 1987).

25. Jean Irigoin, "La terminologie du livre et de l'écriture dans le monde byzantin," in Weijers (ed.), *Vocabulaire du livre,* p. 15.

26. In particular, see in Irigoin, ibid., and articles by Pierre Gasnault, "Les supports et les instruments de l'écriture à l'époque médiévale," ibid., and François Dolbeau, "Noms de livres," ibid.

27. *Tractatus adversus Judaeorum inveterata duritiem*, in *PL*, vol. 189, col. 606. Texts quoted by Gasnault, "Les supports," pp. 25 and 26.

28. According to Varro, quoted by Pliny (*Histoire Naturelle* 13, 70), parchment was invented in Pergamus, in Mysia, during the reign of Eumenius I (197–159 B.C.). Varro uses the word *membrana*. The reference to the city of Pergamus (*pergamena charta*, whence "parchment") came much later; it appears in an edict of Diocletian, in the year 301 where *pergamenum* is a type of parchment, probably the white kind, as opposed to the yellow kind named *crocatum*. See Irigoin, "La terminologie du livre," pp. 15–16.

29. D.41.1.9.1 *Chartis* "de bombyce." See Gasnault, "Les supports," p. 27. The *Siete Partidas* of Alfonso X of Castille, *Las Siete Partidas del sabio rey don Alfonso el nono, nuevamente glosadas por el licenciado Gregorio López* (Salamanca, 1555) (reproduced in *Boletín Oficial del Estado,* 1974), distinguish between *pargamino de paño* (fabric parchment) and *pargamino de cuero* (leather parchment) (3.18.5 "Quales cartas deuen ser fechas de pargamino de cuero, e quales de pargamino de paño": which letters must be made of fabric parchment, and which of leather parchment), the choice of which depends on the contents of the act. The most important ones must be inscribed on leather parchment. López's gloss affirms, relying on Baldus, that this is not "de necessitate esse ad valorem chartae" (necessarily linked to the value of the chart).

30. On this subject, see Elisabeth Lalou (ed.), *Les tablettes à écrire de l'Antiquité à l'époque moderne* (Turnhout, 1992); Richard H. Rouse and Mary A. Rouse, "The Vocabulary of Wax Tablets," in Olga Weijers (ed.), *Vocabulaire du livre,* pp. 220–30.

31. Baudri de Bourgueil, *Poèmes,* vols. 1 and 2, text, translation, and commentary

by Jean-Yves Tilliette (Paris, 1998 and 2002): "Ô nouvelle norme, nouvelle forme, nouvelle race de tablettes! Voici que je tiens dans ma main des tablettes naines" (p. 36). "Accompagnez mon existence; jamais un rustre, un vieillard décrépit ou un galeux ne portera la main sur vous. Le champs que vous constituez ne sera pas labouré par moi un style émoussé et vous ne serez pas rongées par la prolixité vorace. [...] Acceptez-moi pour compagnon privilégié, réjouissons-nous de mêmes joies. Que ma mort, et rien d'autre, nous sépare, moi de vous, vous de moi, et qu'une main compatissante vous installe dans mon tombeau." (p. 123).

32. Rouse and Rouse, "Vocabulary of Wax Tablets," p. 220.

Chapter 2

1. Placentin, *Summa Institutionum* (Mayenz, 1535, reprinted in the *Corpus glossatorum juris civilis* 1 [Turin, 1973]). Peter Weimar, in Helmut Coing (ed.), *Handbuch der Quellen und Literatur der neueren europäischen Privatrechtsgeschichte* I (Munich, 1973), p. 205, mentions the 1170s, but A. Converso, in the introduction to the reprint published in the *Corpus Glossatorum*, pp. iii–ix does not take a position. In any case, the *Summa* was probably written in Montpellier.

2. Azo, *Summa Institutionum* (Lyon, 1564).

3. This passage, which belongs to the *distinctiones* genre, is not recorded by Émile Seckel, *Distinctiones glossatorum* (Berlin, 1911). I owe this piece of information, among many others, to Emanuele Conte, who read a late version of this text, for which I am very thankful.

4. On the issue of drifting trees under Roman law and, in particular, on the opposition between the so-called "principle of the trunk" and "principle of the roots," see Rolph Knütel, "Arbres errants, îles flottantes, animaux fugitifs et trésors enfouis," *Revue d'histoire du droit français et étranger* 76 (1998): 191 ff.

5. In fact, under Justinian law, the *ius alluvionis* seems to designate the *alluvio* as a slow and imperceptible process, as well as the *alveus derelictus*, the *insula in flumine nata*, and the *avulsio*, see Lauretta Maganzani, "Gli incrementi fluviali in Fiorentino VI Inst.," *Studia et Documenta Historiae et Iuris* 59 (1993): 222, n. 61.

6. Azo, *Summa*, I.2.1 *ad* 30, which is reiterated in the ordinary gloss at *Intelligi non possit*.

7. Ibid., *ad* 29. We will see that, in reality, what matters most is the criterion of the agent of *accessio*.

8. Ibid., *ad* 35 to 44.

9. Ibid., *ad* 46.

10. Johannes de Platea (late fourteenth century), *Commentaria in quattuor libros Institutionum . . . , cum additionibus Johannem de Gradibus* (Lyon, 1507), I.2.1.26 *Si tamen*.

11. Tradition assigns four disciples to Irnerius, better known as the four doctors, Martino, Bulgaro, Iacopo, and Ugo, who would have taken part in the Roncaglia Diet of 1158. The first two became very well known, and tradition, in part wrongly, makes them adversaries on the issue of the interpretation of the law (see Cortese, *Il diritto,*

vol. 2, pp. 76–88). They authored numerous glosses. Martino († ca. 1166) in particular was interested in the topic of the *tabula picta*; he was the first to defend the value of writing.

12. "Cassum Sancti Galli Continuatio I auctore Ekkerhardo IV," in *MGH,* SS, II (Hanover, 1829), p. 122. Quoted by Armando Petrucci, "Leer en la Edad Media," in *Alfabetismo, escritura, sociedad* (Barcelona, 1999), p. 186. On the education of scribes in the High Middle Ages, see Armando Petrucci, "Alfabetismo ed educazione grafica degli scribi altomedievali (sec. VII–X)," in P. Ganz (ed.), *The Role of the Book in Medieval Culture,* vol. 1 (Turnhout, 1986), pp. 109–31. See also Françoise Gasparri, "L'enseignement de l'écriture à la fin du Moyen Âge: À propos du *Tractatus in omnem scribendi,* manuscrit 76 de l'Abbaye de Kremsmünster," *Scrittura e civiltà* 3 (1979): 244.

13. Jehan Spencer-Smith (ed.) (Rouen, 1841) and Klaus Arnold (ed.) (Würzburg, 1973). I have not been able to review the edition cited by Armando Petrucci, "Alfabetismo."

14. About collections of model letters and advertising boards of the writing masters, see Françoise Gasparri, "Enseignement et technique de l'écriture du Moyen Âge à la fin du XVIe siècle," *Scrittura e civiltà* 7 (1983): 201–22. According to this author, few treatises about calligraphy from the fourteenth and fifteenth centuries have survived, but they surely follow more ancient models, "L'enseignement de l'écriture," p. 246.

15. This treatise was studied by Francisco M. Gimeno Blay, who edited it: "Una aventura caligráfica: Gabriel Altadell y su 'De arte scribanne' (*ca.* 1468)," *Scrittura e civiltà* 17 (1993): 203–70.

16. Jonathan J. G. Alexander, *Medieval Illuminators and their Methods of Work* (New Haven, Conn., 1992), pp. 4–34.

17. Carla Bozzolo and Ezio Ornato, "Les fluctuations de la production manuscrite à la lumière de l'histoire de la fin du Moyen Âge français," in Ezio Ornato, *La face cachée du livre médiéval: L'histoire du livre vue par Ezio Ornato, ses amis, et ses collègues* (Rome, 1997), p. 184.

18. Albert Derolez, "Pourquoi les copistes signaient-ils leurs manuscrits?" in Emma Condelo and Giuseppe De Gregorio (eds.), *Scribi e colofoni: Le sottoscrizione di copisti dalle origine all'avventa della stampa,* Atti del Seminario de Erice, X Colloquio del Comité International de Paléographie Latine (October 23–28, 1993) (Spoleto, 1995), pp. 37–56. About the signed legal manuscripts, see Franck Soetermeer, "À propos d'une famille de copistes: Quelques remarques sur la librairie à Bologne aux XIIIe et XIVe siècles," in *Livres et juristes au Moyen Âge* (Goldbach, 1999), pp. 95–148, first published in *Studi Medievali,* ser. 3 (1989).

19. See the example given by Guyotjeannin, "Le vocabulaire," p. 126. As to Adelard of Bath, I am referring to his *Quaestiones naturales* edited by Martin Müller, *Die 'quaestiones naturales' des Adelardus von Bath* (Münster, 1934), Beiträge zur Geschichte des Philisophie im Mittelalter, XXXI–2, p. 2. The relationship to painting appears differently in Jean Gerson, since he designates those who copy without the least understanding of the text; see John Gerson, *De laude scriptorum tractatus,* Jehan Spencer-Smith (ed.) (Rouen, 1841), pp. 1–2, quoted by Françoise Gasparri, "Note sur l'enseignement de l'écriture au XVe–XVIe siècles: À propos d'un nouveau placard du XVIe siècle découvert à la Bibliothèque Nationale," *Scrittura e civiltà* 2 (1978): 249.

20. See the chapters Cennino Cennini dedicates to the practice of drawing on

tablets and on parchment or tinted paper, *Il Libro dell'arte*, Franco Brunello (ed.) (Vicenza, 1971). There exists a French translation and criticism by Colette Deroche, *Cennino Cennini: Le livre d'art* (Paris, 1991).

21. Pier Paolo Vergerio, *De ingenuis moribus et liberalibus studiis adulescentiae*, A. Gnesotto (ed.), (1918), quoted by Baxandall, *Giotto and the Orators*, p. 125.

22. Baxandall, *Giotto and the Orators*, p. 135.

23. Alberti, *De Pictura* (1435), translated by Jean Luis Schefer (Paris, 1992), p. 217.

24. This refers to the action of *tignum iunctum*, incorporated beam: I cannot remove it, but nor is there extinction of the object. Wood and construction materials do not cease being, having an individuality, even though, due to public utility, I cannot deform a building by removing the things that belongs to me. On the action of *tignum iunctum* under Roman law, Francesco Musumeci, "Vicenda storica del '*tignum iunctum*,'" *Bolletino dell'Instituto di diritto romano* 81 (1978): 201–65.

25. Paolo da Castro, *Praelectiones Auenionenses in digestum Vetus* (Venice, 1593), D.6.23.2 *Si quis rei*.

Chapter 3

1. Placentin, *Summa*.

2. Du Cange, *Glossarium mediae et infimae latinitatis*, vol. 2 (Paris, 1842).

3. Placentin, *Summa*, p. 26.

4. See Gasnault, "Les supports," p. 31.

5. Charles Reynold Dodwell (ed. and trans.), *Theophilus: The Various Arts. De diversis artibus* (1st ed. 1961; Oxford, 1986), Introduction, pp. XLIII and XLIV in particular.

6. Eleanor Webster Bulatkin, "The Spanish Word 'Matiz': Its Origin and Semantic Evolution in the Technical Vocabulary of Medieval Painters," *Traditio* 10 (1954): 488, quoted by Chiara Garzya Romano, *Eraclio: I colori e le arti dei romani e la compilazione pseudo-eracliana* (Bologna, 1996), p. XL.

7. About drawing in the Middle Ages, see Robert W. Scheller, *Exemplum: Model-Book Drawings and the Practice of Artistic Transmission in the Middle Ages (ca. 900–ca. 1470)* (Amsterdam, 1995).

8. Cennino Cennini, *Il Libro dell'arte*, chap. 103. I quote this work using chapters rather than pages to allow an easy concordance with the critical translation by Déroche, *Cennino Cennini: Le Livre de l'art*.

9. Cennino Cennini, *Il Libro dell'arte*, chaps. 113, 115, 117, 122.

10. Odofredo, *Interpretatio in vndecim primos pandectarum libros* (Lyon, 1550), *Sed et id* (D.6.1.23.3), see Appendix 3.

11. See Gherardo Ortalli, *La peinture infamante du XIIIe au XVIe siècle* (Paris, 1994). About *graffiti*, see Francisco M. Gimeno Blay and María Luz Mandingorra Llavata (eds.), "*Los muros tienen la palabra*": *Materiales para una historia de los graffiti*, II Seminari Internacional d'Estudis sobre la Cultura Escrita (Valencia, 1997).

12. The plaster in question probably corresponds to a stage in the preparation of

a wooden support, which was the stucco application mentioned by some construction trades. See Geneviève Bresc-Bautier, *Artiste, patriciens*, p. 67.

13. Placentin, *Summa*.

14. P. Maffei, *Tabula picta*, p. 52.

15. See Appendix 1. If such is the case, the passage could belong to a commentary on *Vetus*; however, there remains no edition or complete manuscript of such work; only *Additiones ad Digestum vetus* exist in the Vatican and in Modena, which I was unable to review. Yet it could also be an interpretation of Rainiero's *Lectura* to the *Digestus Novus* (Lyon, 1523), D.41.1.9.2.

16. Jean Faure (aka Iohannes de Runcini, Faber, † 1340), a French master, a magistrate for the city of Montpellier and probably a professor in that same city, is mostly famous for his commentary on the *Institutes*.

17. See Appendix 1.

18. Jacques de Révigny is the most prominent member of that school in Orléans, which enjoyed great notoriety during the second half of the thirteenth century. Founded in 1235 by Pope Gregory IX and dedicated to the teaching of Roman law, which his predecessor, Honorius III, had forbidden in Paris, the Orléans school is credited with having introduced the method of scholasticism into the lawyers' practice. Jacques de Révigny taught there between the seventies and nineties of the thirteenth century. Around 1296, he joined the service of Philippe le Bel, and in 1306, he became bishop of Auxerre and chancellor of France. About the Orléans school, see Eduard Maurits Meijers, "L'Université d'Orléans au XIIIᵉ siècle," in his *Études d'histoire du droit*, vol. 3, Robert Feenstra and H. F. W. Fischer (eds.) (Leiden, 1959), pp. 3–148.

19. Johannes Faber, *Commentaria in quatuor lib. Insti.* (Lyon, 1549).

20. See Chapter 8.

21. D.41.1.7.7–8. See Appendix 1.

Chapter 4

1. The word *substantia* is problematic. It could refer to the substrate, perhaps the matter; in any case, it is not used here to mean the essence, the quiddity of the thing.

2. Odofredo, *Praelectiones in postremum Pandectarum Iustiniani Tomum, uulgo Digestum nouum* (Lyon, 1552), D.50.16.14 *Abest*.

3. Ibid., at *Res abesse*.

4. *Summa Theologiae* I, q.76, a.7, in Thomas Aquinas, *Opera omnia* (Editio Leonina), vols. 4–12 (Rome, 1888–1906), quoted by Rudi A. Te Velde, *Participation and Substantiality in Thomas Aquinas* (Leyden, N.Y., 1995), p. 218, n. 11.

5. *Quaestiones disputatae De potentia Dei* q.3, a.16 *ad* 21, in Thomas Aquinas, *Quaestiones Disputatae*, P. Pession (ed.), vol. 2 (Turin, 1965), quoted by Rudi A. Te Velde, *Participation and Substantiality*, p. 219, n. 13. According to this author, this may refer to Boecius's expression in *De Trinitate*, c. 2: "omne namque esse ex forma est" (it is that all being is born of a form). About the centrality of the principle "forma dat esse" in Thomas Aquinas, contrary to statements by authors such as Étienne Gilson and Cornelio Fabro, see pp. 218–44.

6. *De anima* q. un., a. 10.

7. Aristotle, *La Métaphysique*, trans. Jean Tricot, revisited with commentaries (Vrin, 1964): "Finally, the quiddity, expressed in the definition, is also called the substance of each thing" (1017b, 22); "each being, in fact, is not distinguished, it seems, from its own substance, and we call quiddity the substance of each thing" (1031a, 16–17); "the being in the primary sense is 'what the thing is,' a notion that expresses nothing but the substance" (1028a, 13–14).

8. See Chapter 6.

9. Bartolo da Sassoferrato, *Tyberiadis, Tractatus de Fluminibus* (Bologna, 1576), reprint with an introduction by Guido Astuti (Turin, 1964), Pars tertia, *ad Stricta ratione*, pp. 109–15.

10. André Alciat, *De verborum significatione libri quatuor* (Lyon, 1537), fol. 113, about the same excerpt of D.50.16.13 by Ulpian.

11. D.32.1.52.9 *Cedunt*. Rogerius, probably French but trained in Bologna, was regarded by some as the precursor to Placentin in Montpellier; today, that hypothesis has been abandoned and we believe he did not teach in Provence before Placentin did, but in Arles or Saint-Gilles. See André Gouron, "Sur les traces de Rogerius en Provence," in *Liber amicorum: Études offertes à Pierre Jaubert* (Bordeaux, 1992), pp. 313–26.

12. See Appendix 2.

13. See Appendix 2.

Chapter 5

1. Pietro Bonfante, *Corso di diritto romano*, vol. 2, *La proprietà*, I (1926; reprint, Milan, 1966), p. 130.

2. Seneca, *Epistulae morales* III, Books 93–124, Loeb Classical Library, trans. Richard M. Gummere (1925; reprint, Cambridge, Mass.,1989), p. 170, epistle 102, 6, trans. Paul Veyne, *Entretiens, Lettres à Lucilius* (Paris, 1993), p. 991.

3. About stoic influences, Christopher Meister, *De philosophia iuris consultorum romanorum stoica in doctrina de corporibus eorumque partibus* (Göttingen, 1756); Paul Sokolowski, *Die Philosophie im Privatrecht, Sachbegriff und Körper in der klassischen Iurisprudenz u. in der modernen Gesetzgebung* (Halle, 1902), pp. 51 ff. also finds an Aristotelian influence, although affirming that for collective things, jurists rely only on the stoics. Eugène Vernay, *Servius et son école* (Paris, 1909), pp. 90 ff., on the contrary, finds a peripatetic influence that, after Servius, allowed the jurists to expand collective things to include inanimate things. Specifically about collective things, Aldo dell'Oro, *Le cose collettive nel diritto romano* (Milan, 1963).

4. *Adv. Math.* IX, 78 ff. This is Book 1 of *Against the Physicists*. Quoted by Jean-Joël Duhot, *La conception stoïcienne de la causalité* (Paris, 1989), pp. 106–7.

5. *Sextus, Adv. Math.* IX, 81. This second tripartition, which designates *hexis, physis*, and *psyche*, is confirmed in Plutarch, *Stoicorum Veterum Fragmenta* coll. ab Arnim (Leipzig, 1905, 1903; reprint, Stuttgart, 1968), vol. 2, no. 460. See Duhot, *La conception stoïcienne de la causalité*, p. 107.

6. On the importance and the originality of the syntagma "uni nomini subiecta," dell'Oro, *Le case collecttive*, p. 7, n. 31. Vernay, *Servius et son école*, p. 104, points out the incompatibility of the syntagma with stoic thought and its Aristotelian origin.

7. Thomas Aquinas, *In duodecim libros Metaphysicorum Aristotelis expositio*, ed. M. R. Cathala, O.P. and P. Fr. R. M. Spiazzi, O.P. (Turin, 1964), pp. 231 ff., L.V.1. VII.

8. Ibid., L. VIII, 1. II, p. 406.

9. The bibliography on the subject is voluminous; we can first point out, on universality as name and the Roman construction of the city, Yan Thomas, "L'institution civile de la cite," *Le Débat* no. 74 (1993): 23–44. There are two classic books about the Middle Ages, Pierre Michaud-Quentin, *Universitas: Expression du mouvement communautaire dans le Moyen Âge latin* (Paris, 1970), and naturally, as a starting point, Ernst Kantorowicz, *Les deux corps du roi* (1957; reprint, Paris, 1989).

10. Alberico de Rosate, *In primam ff. Veter, Item quaecumque* (D.6.1.23.5); see Appendix 5.

11. We will discuss the opposition *factum-infectum* in the next chapter.

12. Robert B. Todd, *Alexander of Aphrodisias on Stoic Physics: A Study of the De mixtione with Preliminary Essays, Text, Translation and Commentary* (Leyden, N.Y., 1976), pp. 114–17 *De mixtione* 214.

13. See note 2.

14. Todd, *Alexander of Aphrodisias*, pp. 50–51.

15. This first manuscript is D'Alblaing 3, fol. 6 v, Leiden, Bibliotheek der Rijksuniversiteit; the author also revises the manuscript from New Haven, Yale University, Law Library, J. C. 817 no. 1, fol. 151 v, and finally that of Leipzig (Universitätsbibliothek 921, fol. 158); for Ennio Cortese's observations, see *La norma giuridica* (Milan, 1962), II, p. 411, n. 1 and p. 414, n. 1.

16. P. Maffei, *Tabula picta*, p. 53.

17. See Appendix 5.

18. I will, once more, refer the reader to the bibliography in Ennio Cortese, *Il diritto*, vol. 2, p. 423, n. 77.

19. See Appendix 5.

20. See Chapter 6.

21. C. R. Dodwell (ed.), Theophilus, *De diversis artibus*, pp. 137–39, "De clavis."

22. Edition, translation, and commentary by Chiara Garzya Romani, Eraclio, *I colori e le arti dei romani e la compilazione pseudo-eracliana*, pp. 21–22. This fragment actually belongs to Book 3, attributed to pseudo Eraclius. According to Garzya Romani, Eraclius's text dates from the eighth century and was written in northeastern Italy, whereas Book 3 would date from the twelfth to the thirteenth century and was probably written in a French environment.

Chapter 6

1. D.6.1.23.2 *Adiecerit*. Inseparability is linked to the theme of *ferruminatio* and *adplumbatio*.

2. See also the gloss at *Cui aurum*: "fractum omnino collisum, et sic vitiatum,

vt eo vti commode non possimus" (completely dented and damaged to the point of being impossible to use conveniently).

3. The Lyon edition of 1627 reads "*rudem.*"

4. Bartolo da Sassoferrato, *In secundam Inforiati Partem Commentaria* (Turin, 1574), D.32.1.78.4.

5. Book 9, 7 1049 a 18–22 of the *Metaphysics* (trans. Hugh Tredennick) (Cambridge, 1933), a similar argument in 7,3 245 b 9 of the *Physics*.

6. Thomas Aquinas, *In duodecim libros Metaphysicorum Aristotelis expositio*, ed. M. R. Cathala, O.P. and P. Fr. R. M. Spiazzi, O.P. (Turin, 1964), pp. 440, L. IX. 1. VI.

7. Odofredo, *Interpretatio in undecim primos, Item quacumque* (D.6.1.23.5). See Appendix 3.

8. *In Primam ff Veteris, Si quis rei suae* (D.6.1.23.2). See Appendix 5.

9. Alberico de Rosate, *In primam ff Veteris, Item quaecumque* (D.6.1.23). See Appendix 5.

10. D.32.70.1 *Facta.*

Chapter 7

1. Ferrini, "Appunti sulla dottrina," in particular pp. 69–70.

Chapter 8

1. Enrico Besta, *L'opera d'Irnerio (Contributo alla Storia del diritto italiano)*, II, *Glosse inedite al Digestum Vetus* (Turin, 1896), p. 82.

2. The Stockholm manuscript, Kungliga Bibliotek, B 680, f.75ra contains two glosses signed "y" which confirm the principle by which painting, like writing, appertains to that without which it cannot subsist. P. Maffei, *Tabula picta*, p. 19.

3. Gustav Hänel, *Dissensiones dominorum sive controversiae veterum iuris romani interpretum qui glossatores vocatur* (Leipzig, 1834), pp. 35–36, § 50.

4. Cennino Cennini, *Il Libro dell'arte*, chap. 96.

5. Alberti, *De Pictura*, pp. 152–53, and 158–59.

6. Ibid., pp. 164–65.

7. Ibid., pp. 94–95 refers to those debates, even if Alberti does not regard them as useful to the painter.

8. *Epistola ad Candidum Decembrem* by Valla, published in *Opera* (Basel, 1540), pp. 639–41, quoted and translated by Michael Baxandall, *Les humanistes*, pp. 142–45 and 233–36. This incident may have caused Valla to leave Padua in 1433; it is part of the violent dispute between humanists and jurists mostly faithful to the tradition of the gloss and commentary writers.

9. Bartolo da Sassoferrato, *Tractatus de insigniis et armis*, included in Baldus de Ubaldis, *Tractatus de quaestionibus* (Paris, 1475), fol. 31v–32v.

10. An Arab scholar known in the West under the name Alhacen (or Alhazen);

he wrote his seven-book optics treatise shortly before 1030. It was to be translated into Latin around the 1200s and became known under the names *Perpectiva* or *De aspectibus*. Its influence was enormous.

11. On this question, see Gérard Simon, *Archéologie de la vision: L'optique, le corps, la peinture* (Paris, 2002), pp. 118 ff.

12. Witelo, *Opticae libri decem*, included in Ibn al-Haitham, *Opticae thesaurus*, Friedrich Risner (ed.) (Basel, 1572), vol. 2, p. 184. Witelo's treatise dates from ca. 1270.

13. Katherine Tachau, *Vision and Certitude in the Age of Ockham: Optics, Epistemology and the Foundation of Semantics 1250–1345* (Leiden, 1988), p. 8.

14. See *De multiplicatione specierum*, David Lindberg (ed.), *Roger Bacon's Philosophy of Nature: A Critical Edition, Introduction and Notes of De multiplicatione specierum and De speculis comburentibus* (Oxford, 1983), I, i, l. 23–29, quoted by Tachau, *Vision and Certitude*, p. 8.

15. Azo, *Summa*, see Chapter 2.

16. According to Tamassia, "Odofredo," p. 383, it was more likely a document in favor of Ravenna's metropolitan.

17. See Appendix 3.

18. On the colors, their preparation, their relative cost, and their qualities, see the treatise by Cennino Cennini, *Il Libro dell'arte.*, chap. 29 ff.

19. Bartolo da Sassoferrato, *In primam Digesti Novi Partem,* Commentaria (Turin, 1574), D.41.1.9.

20. Bartolo da Sassoferrato, *In primam Digesti Verteri Partem,* Commentaria (Turin, 1574), D.6.1.23.3–4.

21. Johannes Faber, *Commentaria in quatuor.*

22. Alberico de Rosate, *In primam Digesti Veteris, Sed et id* (D.6.1.23.3).

23. In the ordinary gloss, Book 3, Title 40 of Gregory IX's *Decretales, De consecratione ecclesiae vel altaris*, at X.3.40.1, *Altare*, at the end: "Sacrum trahit ad se non sacrum." In the gloss, at X. 3.40.3, *consecrato*: "Et ita sacrum tanquam dignius trahit ad se non sacrum" (and thus what is sacred, being more dignified, attracts what is not sacred), Gregory IX, *Decretals . . . cum glossis* (Venice, 1605).

Chapter 9

1. Bonfante, *Corso di diritto romano*, p. 160.

2. Baldus de Ubaldi, *Commentaria in primam et secundam partem FF veteris* (Lyon, 1517), D.6.1 *De rei vendi.*

3. Bartolo da Sassoferrato, *In secundam Digesti Novi Partem Commentaria*, D.50.16.25 (Turin, 1574).

4. Bartolo da Sassoferrato, *In secundam Infortiati Partem Commentaria*, D.32.1.89 *Re coniucti* n. 10 (Turin, 1574).

5. I say "suppose" because, while reading his commentary at D.50.16.25 *Recte dicastères*, one realizes that the same entity should be understood, depending on the circumstances, as a universal or integral whole. Bartolo da Sassoferrato, *In secundam Digesti Novi* (Turin, 1574).

6. I owe the information about the scholastic texts to the kindness and generosity of Marie-Pierre Gaviano. Duns Scot, particularly in his *Expositio in Metaphysica Aristotelis*, mentions a series of *partes* (*pars formalis-materialis, formalis-substantialis, homogenea-heterogenea, propincua-remota, proprie-improprie dicta, reales-rationis*) that illustrate this proliferation associated to metaphysics. See Mariano Fernández García, *Lexicon scholasticum philosophico-theologicum* (Hildesheim, 1988, 1910), pp. 464–66. The texts of logic, such as Peter of Spain's *Summulae logicales*, which, from the thirteenth century, will become one of the most famous logic textbooks, deal with the integrating and subjective parts, *in modo, in tempore, in loco*. His commentator Versorius adds five more (*copulativum, disjuntivum, potestativum, successivum, collectivum*), which can be linked to the first two. See Petrus Hispanus, *Summulae logicales cum Versorii parisienses clarísima expositione* (Hildesheim, 1981; Venice facsimile, 1572).

7. Alberico de Rosate, *Dictionarium iuris* (Turin, 1519), fol. 220.

8. Jason of Mayno (1435–1519) taught for most of his life in Padua, where Andrea Alciato (1492–1550) became his pupil. He is the last great professor who wrote a monumental *lectura* to the *Digeste* and the *Codex*.

9. Jason of Mayno, *In Secundam Infortiati partem Commentaria* (Venice, 1573), D.30.1.30 rubr. nu 10.

10. The *Dictionarium* refers to D.25.4.1.1 in "*De inspiciendo ventre custodiandoque partu.*" About this conception, associated with the manner in which the stoics conceive of the child to be born, see Yan Thomas, "El vientre: Cuerpo materno y derecho paterno," in *Los artificios de las instituciones: Estudios de derecho romano* (Buenos Aires, 1999), pp. 125–50.

11. Alberico de Rosate, *Dictionarium*, fol. 220, "De adornante ut testes sunt pars corporis."

12. "Similitudinaria ff. de usufructus in multis (D.7.1.4)," ibid. It is, in fact, a law that states, "Usufructus in multis casibus pars dominij est" (in numerous cases, the usufruct is a part of the property) and the unsigned gloss *Pars dominij* explains the difference between *dominium*, which is "quoddam totum continens sub se proprietatem nudam, et usufructum" (a sort of whole including the bare property and its usufruct) and the "*proprietas nuda.*"

13. "Ut adscripti eius glebae C. de agricol. et censi. l ii (C.11.48.2 vulgata 11.47)," which deals with the serf *inhaerens* to the land, and states one cannot sell a land without transferring the serfs along with it, unless a pact to that effect is obtained. See *Vocabularium iurisprudentiae romanae* (Berlin, 1914), vol. 4, col. 493–513.

14. Pierre Legendre, "*La Summa Institutionum 'Iustiniani est in hoc opere.' Manuscrit Pierpont Morgan 903*," *Ius Commune*, Sonderhefte 2 (Frankfurt am Main, 1973).

15. André Gouron, "Die Enstehung des französischen Rechtsschule: Summa 'Iustiniani est in hoc opere' und Tübinger Rechtsbuch," *Zeitschrift der Savigny-Stiftung für Rechtsgeschichte*, Rom. Abt., 93 (1976): 138–60, now in *La Science du droit dans le Midi de la France au Moyen Âge* (London, 1984), IX.

16. Legendre, "*La Summa Institutionum,*" p. 48.

Chapter 10

1. Bartolo da Sassoferrato, *In secundam Infortiati.*, D.34.2.21.
2. Paolo da Castro, *Praelectiones Auenionenses in digestum Vetus* (Venice, 1593), *Si quis rei* (D.6.23.2).
3. *In primam Digesti Veteris, Item cuaecumque* (D.6.1.23).
4. Trained in Bologna and Naples, Jacobo de Belviso (1270–ca. 1335) settled in Perugia in the year the *studium* was founded (1308). About this author, see Domenico Maffei, *Giuristi medievali e falsificazione editoriali del primo Cinquecento: Iacopo de Belviso in Provenza?, Ius commune*, Sonderhefte 10 (Frankfurt am Main, 1979).
5. About things that are accessory in Roman law and in the work of the commentators, see Piero Rasi, *La pertinenze e le cose accessorie* (Padua, 1955), in particular, pp. 150–215.
6. Alberico de Rosate, *In Secundam Infortiati Partem Commentarij* (Venice, 1586), *Perueniamus* (D.34.2.19.13).
7. From Lodi, trained in Bologna and a professor at various *studia*, Oldrado da Ponte Laude (✝ 1335) became an advisor to John XXII in Avignon and was very influential in papal politics; see Chiara Valsecchi, *Oldrado da Ponte e i suoi consilia: Un'auctoritas del primo trecento* (Milan, 2000).

Chapter 11

1. Angelo de Ubaldi, *Lectura super prima parte FF. veteris* (Milan, 1477), *Si quis* (D.6.1.23.2)
2. Ibid., *Sed et id quod* (D.6.1.23.3).
3. From the context, it seems the word should be read *"ornamentalis."*
4. Johannes de Platea, *Commentaria in quattuor.*, I.2.1.33.

Conclusion

1. Jean-Claude Bonne, "Entre l'image et la matière: la choséité du sacré en Occident," in Jean-Marie Sansterre and Jean-Claude Schmitt (eds.), *Les images dans les sociétés médiévales: Pour une histoire comparée, Bulletin de l'Institut Historique Belge de Rome* 69 (1999): 77–111.
2. See Cortese, *Il diritto*, vol. 2, p. 142.
3. See *Tractatus de fluminibus*.
4. *L'auteur, propriétaire de son oeuvre? La formation du droit d'auteur du XVIe siècle à la loi de 1957*, Ph.D. diss. in law, Université Robert Schuman (Strasbourg III), 1999.
5. On the function of *dominium Dei* in the origination of the modern concept of ownership, see Marie-France Renoux-Zagamé, *Origines théologiques du concept moderne de propriété* (Geneva, 1987).

6. Hermann Hagen, *Anecdota Helvetica quae ad grammaticam latinam spectant*, in Heinrich Keil, *Grammatici latini*, vol. 8 (Leipzig, 1870; reprint, Hildesheim, 1961), pp. 302–7.

7. On the relationship between writing and image in Gregory the Great, see Jean-Claude Schmitt, "Écriture et image," in *Le corps*, pp. 97–133, first published in Emmanuèle Baumgarter and Christiane Marchello-Nizia (eds.), *Théories et pratiques de l'écriture au Moyen Âge* (Paris, 1988). According to the author, this hierarchy "is subjected to the growing and continuous pressure of the image" (p. 131).

Appendixes

1. The word may refer to the second bark of the linden tree or to the strip of papyrus.

2. The *codices eborei* are probably the ivory diptychs and polyptychs written in ink. See Wilhelm Wattenbach, *Das Schriftwesen im Mittelalter* (Leipzig, 1875), pp. 45 and 53, quoted by Gasnault, "Les supports," p. 23.

3. This word refers to the gluing of sheets in sequence to make a roll. See Jean Vezin, "Le vocabulaire latin de la reliure au Moyen Âge," in Weijers (ed.), *Vocabulaire du livre*, p. 56.

Bibliography

Primary Sources

Aegidius Romanus. *Commentaria in octo libros Physicorum Aristotelis.* 1502.

Alberico de Rosate. *Dictionarium iuris.* Turin, 1519.

———. *In primam ff. Veter. Part. Commentarij.* Venice, 1585

———. *In secundam Infortiati Partem Commentarij.* Venice, 1586

Alberti. *De Pictura.* 1435. Trans. Jean Luis Schefer. Paris, 1992

Alphonse X the Wise. *Las Siete Partidas del sabio rey don Alfonso el nono, nuevamente glosadas por el licenciado Gregorio López.* Salamanca, 1555. Reprint, *Boletín Oficial del Estado*, 1974.

André Alciat. *De verborum significatione libri quatuor.* Lyon, 1537.

Angelo de Ubaldi. *Lectura super prima parte FF. veteris.* Milan, 1477.

Aristotelis opera cum Averrois commentariis. Vol. 4, *De physico auditu.* Venice, 1562.

Azo. *Summa Institutionum.* Lyon, 1564.

Baldus de Ubaldi. *Commentaria in primam et sucundam partem FF veteris.* Lyon, 1517.

Bartolo da Sassoferrato. *In primam Digesti Novi Partem Commentaria.* Turin, 1574.

———. *In primam Digesti Veteri Partem Commentaria.* Turin, 1574.

———. *In secundam Digesti Novi Partem Commentaria.* Turin, 1574.

———. *In secundam Infortiati Partem Commentaria.* Turin, 1574.

———. *Tractatus de insigniis et armis.* In Baldus de Ubaldi, *Tractatus de quaestionibus.* Paris, 1475.

———. Tyberiadis, *Tractatus de fluminibus.* Bologna, 1576. Reprint with an introduction by Guido Astuti, Turin, 1964.

Baudri de Bourgeuil. *Poèmes.* Ed., trans., and commentary by Jean-Yves Tilliette. Paris, vol. 1, 1998; vol. 2, 2002.

Besta Enrico (ed.). *L'opera d'Irnerio (Contributo alla Storia del diritto italiano),* II. *Glosse inedite al digestum Vetus.* Turin, 1896.

Cennino Cennini. *Il Libro dell'arte.* Ed. Franco Brunello. Vicenza, 1971. French critical translation by Colette Déroche. *Cennino Cennini: Le Livre de l'art.* Paris, 1991.

Chartularium Studii Bononiensis. Documenti per la storia dell'Università di Bologna dalle origini sino al secolo XV. 15 vols. Bologna, 1909–88.

Dissensiones dominorum sive controversiae veterum iuris romani interpretum qui glossatores vocatur. Ed. Hänel Gustav. Leipzig, 1834.

Duns Scot. *In VIII libros physicorum Aristotelis quaestiones, Opera omnia,* vol. 2. Paris, 1891.

Eraclio. *I colori e le arti dei romani e la compilazione pseudo-eracliana.* Ed. Chiara Garzya Romano. Bologna, 1996.

Grégoire IX. *Decretales . . . cum glossis.* Venice, 1605.

Guillaume d'Ockham. *Quaestiones in libros physicorum Aristotelis, Opera philosophica,* vol. 6. New York, 1984.

Guillaume Durand. *Rationale divinorum officiorum.* Ed. A. Davril O.S.B. and T. M. Thibodeau. *Corpus Christianorum, Continuatio Mediaeualis,* 140. Turnhout, 1995.

Hage, Hermann (ed.). *Anecdota Helvetica quae ad grammaticam latinam spectant.* In Heinrich Keil, *Grammatici latini,* vol. 8. Leipzig, 1870. Reprint, Hildesheim, 1961.

Jason de Mayno. *In Secundam Infortiati partem Commentaria.* Venice, 1573.

Jean Gerson. *De laude scriptorum tractatus.* Ed. Jehan Spencer-Smith. Rouen, 1841.

Johannes de Platea. *Commentaria in quattuor libros Institutionum . . . cum additionibus Johannem de Gradibus.* Lyon, 1507.

Johannes Faber. *Commentaria in quatuor lib. Insti.* Lyon, 1549.

Johannes Trithemius. *De laude scriptorum: Zum Lobe des Schreiber.* Ed. Klaus Arnold. Würtzburg, 1973.

Justinian. *Corpus iuris civilis.* Lyon, 1627.

———. *Digestum infortiatum, cum glossa.* Venice, 1494.

———. *Digestum novum, cum glossa.* Venice, 1477.

———. *Digestum vetus, cum glossa.* Perugia, 1476.

———. *Institutiones, cum apparatu.* Ferrara, 1473.

Legendre, Pierre. "*La Summa Institutionum 'Iustiniani est in hoc opere.' Manuscrit Pierpont Morgan 903.*" *Ius commune,* Sonderhefte 2. Frankfurt am Main, 1973.

Leo Speluncanus. *Artis notaraie tempestatis huius speculum.* Venice, 1575.

Odofredo. *Interpretatio in vndecim primos pandectarum libros.* Lyon, 1550.

———. *Praelectiones in postremum Pandectarum Iustiniani Tomum, uulgo Digestum nouum.* Lyon, 1552.

Paolo da Castro. *Praelectiones Auenionenses in digestum Vetus.* Venice, 1593.

Paul. *Sententiae, Corpus Iuris Romani Anteiustiniani,* vol. 1. Bologna, 1837. Reprint, Aalen, 1987.

Petrus Hispanus. *Summulae logicales cum versorii parisienses clarísima expositione.* Hildesheim, 1981. Venice facsimile, 1572.

Placentin. *Summa Institutionum.* Mayence, 1535. Reprint in *Corpus glossatorum juris civilis* 1, Turin, 1973.

Rainiero Arsendi da Forlì. *Lectura super digesto novo.* Lyon, 1563. Reprint, *Opera iuridica rariora,* vol. 9, Bologna, 1968.

Rainiero de Perugia. *Ars notaria.* In *Scripta anecdota antiquissimorum glossatorum,* ed. Augusto Gaudenzi. *Bibliotheca Iuridica Medii Aevi II.* Bologna, 1892.

Rolandino Passaggeri. *Summa totius artis notariae Rolandini Rodulphini Bononiensis vir praestantissimi eandem summam luculentissimus apparatus, qui Aurora per excellentiam dicitur . . . .* Venice, 1546.

Seneca. *Entretiens. Lettres à Lucilius.* Trans. Paul Veyne. Paris, 1993.

———. *Epistulae morales III,* Books 93–124. Loeb Classical Library. Trans. Richard M. Gummere. 1925. Reprint, Cambridge, Mass., 1989.

Théophile, Theophilus. *De diversis artibus. The Various Arts.* Ed. and trans. Charles R. Dodwell. 1961. Oxford, 1986.
Thomas Aquinas, *In duodecim libros Metaphysicorum Aristotelis expositio.* Ed. M. R. Cathala, O.P. and P. Fr. R. M. Spiazzi, O.P. Turin-Rome, 1964.
Witelo. *Opticae libri decem.* In Ibn al-Haitham, *Optiacae thesaurus,* ed. Friedrich Risner. Vol. 2. Basel, 1572.

Secondary Sources

Alexander, Jonathan J. G. *Medieval Illuminators and Their Methods of Work.* New Haven, Conn., 1992.
Arangio-Ruiz, Vincenzo. *Istituzione di diritto romano.* Naples, 1974.
Bartolo da Sassoferrato. Studi e documenti per il IV centenario. 2 vols. Milan, 1962.
Baxandall, Michael. "Les conditions du marché." In *L´oeil du Quatttrocento.* 1972. Reprint, Paris, 1985.
———. *Giotto and the Orators: Humanist Observers of Painting in Italy and the Discovery of Pictorial Composition: 1350–1450.* Oxford, 1971.
Bonfante, Pietro. *Corso di diritto romano.* Vol. 2, *La proprietà,* I. 1926. Milan, 1966.
Bouza Alvarez, Fernando. *Corre manuscrito: Una historia cultural del Siglo de Oro.* Madrid, 2001.
Bozolo, Carla, and Ezio Ornato. "Les fluctuations de la production manuscrite à la lumière de l'histoire de la fin du Moyen Âge français." In Ezio Ornato, *La face cachée du livre médiéval: L'histoire du livre vue par Ezio Ornato, ses amis et ses collègues,* pp. 179–95. Rome, 1997.
Branca, Guiseppe. "Accessione." In *Encyclopedia del diritto,* vol. 1, pp. 261–72. Milan, 1958.
Bresc-Bautier, Geneviève. *Artiste, patriciens et confréries: Production et consommation de l'œuvre d'art à Palerme et en Sicile occidentale (1348–1460).* Rome, 1979.
Calasso, Francesco. *Medio Evo del diritto: I. Le fonti.* Milan, 1954.
Caprioli, Severino. *Indagini sul Bolognini: Giurisprudenza e filologia nel quattrocento italiano.* Milan, 1969.
Chartier, Roger. "Figures de l'auteur." In *Culture écrite et société: L'ordre des libres (XIVᵉ–XVIIIᵉ siècles),* pp. 45–80. Paris, 1996.
Coing, Helmut (ed.). *Handbuch der Quellen und Literatur der neueren europäischen Privatrechtsgeschichte I.* Munich, 1973.
Cortese, Ennio. *Il diritto nella storia medievale.* 2 vols. Rome, 1995–96.
———. *Il rinascimento giuridico medievale.* Rome, 1992.
Dell'oro Aldo. *Le cose collecttive nel diritto romano.* Milan, 1963.
Denifle, Henri. "Die Statuten der Juristen-Universität Bologna vom J. 1317–1347, und deren Verhältniss zu jenen Paduas, Perugias, Florenz." *Archiv für Literatur- und Kirchengeschichte des Mittelalters* 3 (1887): 196–493.
Derolez, Albert. "Pourquoi les copistes signaient-ils leurs manuscrits?" In *Scribi e colofoni: Le sottoscrizioni di copisti dalle origini all'avvento della stampa,* Atti del seminario di Erice. X Colloquio del Comité international de paléographie latine

(October 23–28, 1993), ed. Emma Condela and Giuseppe De Gregorio, pp. 37–56. Spoleto, 1995.

Devoti, Luciana. "Aspetti dell produzione del libro a Bologna: Il prezzo di copia del manoscritto giuridico tra XIII e XIV secolo." *Scrittura e civiltà* 18 (1994): 77–142.

Dolbeau, François. "Noms de libres." In *Vocabulaire du livre et de l'écriture au Moyen Âge,* Actes de la table ronde, Paris, September 24–26, 1987, ed. Olga Weijers, pp. 79–99. Turnhout, 1989.

Fernandez García, Mariano. *Lexicon scholasticum philosophico-theologicum.* 1910. Hildesheim, 1988.

Ferrini, Contardo. "Appunti sulla dottrina della specificazione." In *Opere,* vol. 4, pp. 44–112. Milan, 1930. 1st ed. *Bulletino del Istituto di Diritto Romano* 2 (1889).

Filippi, Francesco, and Guido Zucchini. *Miniatori e pittori a Bologna: Documenti dei secoli XIII e XIV.* Florence, 1947.

Foucault, Michel. "Qu'est-ce qu'un auteur?" *Bulletin de la société française de philosophie* 64, no. 22 (1969): 73–104. Included in *Dits et écrits: 1954–1988,* ed. Daniel Defert and Françoise Ewald, with the collaboration of Jacques Lagrange, vol. 1, pp. 789–821. Paris, 1994.

Gasnault, Pierre. "Les supports et les instruments de l'écriture à l'époque médiévale." In Olga Weijers (ed.), *Vocabulaire du livre,* pp. 20–33.

Gasparri, Françoise. "Enseignement et technique de l'écriture du Moyen Âge à la fin du XVIᵉ siècle." *Scrittura e civiltà* 7 (1983): 201–22.

———. "L'enseignement de l'écriture à la fin du Moyen Âge: À propos du *Tractatus in omnem modum scribendi,* manuscrit 76 de l'Abbaye de Kremsmünster." *Scrittura e civiltà* 3 (1979): 243–65.

———. "Note sur l'enseignement de l'écriture aux XVᵉ–XVIᵉ siècles: À propos d'un nouveau placard du XVIᵉ siècle découvert à la Bibliothèque nationale." *Scrittura e civiltà* 2 (1978): 245–61.

Gimeno Blay, Francisco M. "Una aventura caligráfica: Gabriel Altadell y su 'De arte scribendi' (*ca.* 1468)." *Scrittura e civiltà* 17 (1993): 203–70.

Gimeno Blay, Francisco M., and María Luz Mandingorra Llavata (eds.). *"Los muros tienen la palabra": Materiales para una historia de los graffitti.* Il Seminari Internacional d'Estudis sobre la Cultura Escrita. Valence, 1997.

Gouron, André. "Die Entstehung der französischen Rechtsschule: Summa 'Iustiniani est in hoc opere' und Tübinger Rechtsbuch." *Zeitschrift der Savigny-Stiftung für Rechtsgeschichte.* In *La Science du droit dans le Midi de la France au Moyen Âge.* London, 1984.

———. *La Science du droit dans le Midi de la France au Moyen Âge* [Variorum]. London, 1984.

———. "Sur les traces de Rogerius en Provence." In *Liber amicorum: Études offertes à Pierre Jaubert,* pp. 313–26. Bordeaux, 1992.

Guyotjeannin, Olivier. "Le vocabulaire de la diplomatique en latin médiéval." In Olga Weijirs (ed.), *Vocabulaire du livre,* pp. 120–34.

Impallomeni, Gianbattista. "Specificazione." In *Enciclopedia del diritto,* vol. 43, pp. 267–70. Milan, 1990.

Irigoin, Jean. "La terminologie du livre et de l'écriture dans le monde byzantin." In Olga Weijirs (ed.), *Vocabulaire du livre,* pp. 11–19.

Kantorowicz, Ernst. *Les deux corps du roi*. 1957. Paris, 1989.

Knütel, Rolph. "Arbres errants, îles flottantes, animaux fugitifs et trésors enfouis." *Revue d'histoire du droit* 76 (1998): 187–214.

Lalou, Elisabeth (ed.). *Les tablettes à écrire de l'Antiquité à l'époque moderne*. Turnhout, 1992.

Lange, Hermann. *Römisches Recht im Mittelalter, Bd. 1: Die Glossatoren*. Munich, 1997.

Lombardi, Luigi. *Dalla "fides" alla "bona fides."* Milan, 1961.

Love, Harold. *The Culture and Commerce of Texts: Scribal Publication in Seventeenth-century England*. 1993. Amherst, Mass., 1998.

Lucrezi, Francesco. *La* tabula picta *tra creatore e fruitore*. Naples, 1984.

Maddalena, Paolo. "*Accedere* e *cedere* nelle fonti classiche." *Labeo* 17 (1971).

Maffei, Domenico. *Giuristi medievali e falsificazioni editoriali del primo Cinquecento: Iacopo de Belviso in Provenza?, Ius comune*, Sonderhefte 10. Frankfurt am Main, 1979.

———. *Gli inizi dell'umanesimo giuridico*. Milan, 1956.

Maffei, Paola. *Tabula picta: Pittura e scrittura nel pensiero dei glossatori*. Milan, 1988.

Manganzani, Lauretta. "Gli incrementi fluviali in Fiorentino VI *Inst.*" *Studia et Documenta Historiae et Iuris* 59 (1993): 207–58.

Meijers, Eduard Maurits. "L'Université d'Orléans au XIIIᵉ siècle." In *Études d'histoire du droit*, vol. 3, ed. Robert Feenstra and H. F. W. Fischer, pp. 3–148. Leiden, 1959.

Meister, Christopher. *De philosophia iuris consultorum romanorum stoica in doctrina de corporibus eorumque partibus*. Göttingen, 1756.

Michaud-Quantin, Pierre. "Les champs sémantiques de *species*: Tradition latine et traduction du grec." In *Études sur le vocabulaire philosophique du Moyen Âge*, with the collaboration of Michel Lemoine, pp. 113–50. Rome, 1970.

———. *Universitas. Expression du mouvement communautaire dans le Moyen Âge latin*. Paris, 1970.

Milanesi, Gaetani. *Documenti per la storia dell'arte senese*. 3 vols. Sienna, 1854.

Musumeci, Francesco. "Vicenda storica del 'tignum iunctum.'" *Bollettino dell'Istituto di diritto romano* 81 (1978): 201–65.

Orlandelli, Gianfranco. *Il libro a Bologna dal 1300 al 1330: Documenti con uno studio su il contratto di scrittura nella dottrina bolognese*. Bologna, 1959.

Ortalli, Gherardo. *La peinture infamante du XIIIᵉ au XVIᵉ siècle*. 1979. Paris, 1994.

Osuchowski, Waclaw. "Des études sur les modes d'acquisition de la propriéte en droit romain: Recherche sur l'auteur de la théorie éclectique en matière de spécification." In *Studi in onore di Vincenzo Arangio-Ruiz nel XLV anno del suo insegnamento, III*, pp. 37–50. Naples, 1953.

Petrucci, Armando. "Copisti e libri manoscritti dopo l'avvento della stampa." In Emma Condello and Giuseppe De Gregorio (eds.), *Scribi e colofoni*, pp. 507–25.

———. "Dal libro unitario al libro miscellaneo." In Andrea Giardina (ed.), *Società e impero tardoantico. Vol. 4, Tradizioni dei classici, transformazioni della cultura*, pp. 173–87. Bari, 1986.

Pfister, Laurent. *L'auteur, propriétaire de son oeuvre? La formation du droit d'auteur du XVIᵉ siècle à la loi de 1957*. Ph.d. diss. in law, Université Strasbourg III, 1999.

Piano Mortari, Vincenzo. *Diritto, logica, metodo nel secolo XVI*. Naples, 1978.

Renoux-Zagamé, Marie France. *Origines théologiques du concept moderne de propriété.* Geneva, 1987.

Rose, Mark. *Authors and Owners: The Invention of Copyright.* Cambridge, Mass., 1993.

Rouse, Richard H., and Mary A. Rouse. "The Vocabulary of Wax Tablets." In Olga Weijers (ed.), *Vocabulaire du livre,* pp. 220–30.

Scheller, Robert W. *Exemplum: Model-book Drawings and the Practice of Artistic Transmission in the Middle Ages (ca. 900–ca. 1470).* Amsterdam, 1995.

Schmitt, Jean-Claude. *Le corps des images: Essais sur la culture visuelle au Moyen Âge.* Paris, 2002.

Seckel, Émile. *Distinctiones glossatorum.* Berlin, 1911.

Soetemeer, Franck. "La carcerazione del copista." In *Livres et juristes au Moyen Âge,* pp. 191–227. Goldbach, 1999. First published in *Rivista Internazionale di Diritto Comune* 6 (1991).

———. "À propos d'une famille de copistes: Quelques remarques sur la librairie à Bologne aux XIIIᵉ et XIVᵉ siècles." In *Livres et juristes,* pp. 95–148. First published in *Studi Medievali* ser. 3, 30 (1989).

Sokolowski, Paul. *Die philosophie im Privatrecht, Sachbegriff und Körper in der klassischen Iurisprudenz u. in der modernen Gesetzgebung.* Halle, 1902.

Tachau, Katherine. *Vision and Certitude in the Age of Ockham: Optics, Epistemology and the Foundation of Semantics, 1250–1345.* Leiden, 1988.

Talamanca, Mario. "Lo schema *genus species* nelle sistematiche dei giuristi romani." Colloquio italo-francese, April 14–17, 1973. *La filosofia greca e il diritto romano.* Vol. 2. Rome, 1977.

Tamassia, Nino. "Odofredo: Studio storico-giuridico." In *Scritti di storia giuridica,* vol. 2, pp. 335–464. Padua, 1967. First published in *Atti e Memorie Deputazione di Storia patria per la Romagna,* 1894.

Thomas, Yan. "L'institution civile de la cité." *Le Débat* 74 (1993): 23–44.

———. "La valeur des choses." *Annales. Histoire, Sciences Sociales* (November–December 2002): 1431–62.

——. "El vientre: El Cuerpo materno y derecho paterno." In *Los artificios de las instituciones: Estudios de derecho romano,* pp. 125–50. Buenos Aires, 1999.

Todd, Robert B. *Alexander of Aphrodisias on Stoic Physics: A Study of the De mixtione with Preliminary Essays, Text, Translation and Commentary.* Leyden, N.Y., 1976.

Troje, Hans E. *Graeca leguntur: Die Aneignung des byzantinischen Rechts und die Entstehung eines humanisation 'Corpus juris civilis' in der Jurisprudenz des 16. Jahrhunderts.* Cologne, 1971.

Valsecchi, Chiara. *Oldrado da Ponte e i suoi consilia: Un'auctoritas del primo trecento.* Milan, 2000.

Velde, Rudi A. Te. *Participation and Substantiality in Thomas Aquinas.* Leiden, 1995.

Vernay, Eugène. *Servius et son école.* Paris, 1909.

Vocabularium iurisprudentiae romanae. Vol. 4. Berlin, 1914.

Weimar, Peter. "Die legistische Literatur und die Methode des Rechtsunterrichts der Glossatorenzeit." *Ius commune* 2 (1969): 43–83.

Wirth, Jean. *L'image médiévale: Naissance et développement (VIᵉ–XVᵉ siècle).* Paris, 1989.

Index

Acknowledgments

This book could not have been written without the faithful support of several colleagues and institutions. Jacques Revel, Bernard Vincent, and Roger Chartier invited me on several occasions to the École des Hautes Études en Sciences Sociales, where I was able to present various stages in the development of this research project, as well as the other works brought to fruition thanks to the Paris libraries. Georges Martin welcomed me in his research group at Université Paris XIII between 1998 and 2000; Maurice Aymard generously offered the support of Maison des Sciences de l'Homme. I also was awarded a René Thalmann scholarship from Buenos Aires University in 1997, which allowed me to work with Claude Gauvard at Université Paris I. The Universidad Nacional General Sarmiento always gracefully tolerated my research stays abroad, and thus supported work that Argentine public universities could not otherwise have supported.

I am indebted to many colleagues and friends but, in a certain way, the person who is essentially at the origin of this book is Yan Thomas. As this English version was being prepared, Yan Thomas died prematurely. He had an erudite, generous, and sparkling intelligence, and his death has left in me, as in so many others who have read or heard him, a sense of irreparable loss.

I would also like to thank the readers and reading audiences, whose remarks and suggestions have been a precious help year after year. I am in particular debt to Étienne Anheim, Marie-Béatrice Bouger, Fernando Bouza, Roger Chartier, Emanuele Conte, Pierre-Antoine Fabre, Antonia Fiori, Marie-Pierre Gaviano, Alain and Anita Guerreau, and Jean-Claude Schmitt, as well as Jerry Singerman, who accepted this book at the University of Pennsylvania Press, and Dascha Inciarte and David Valayre, who did the translation.

For other, no less fundamental, reasons, I also thank Ruth Arbiser, Gastón Burucúa, Karen Dybner-Madero, Carmiña Escrigas, Sandra Gayol, Roberto Madero, Vittorio Minardi, and Aurora Schreiber, as well as Carlota and Sasha, who are, for me, life itself.